# SALES MANAGEMENT

**Dr. R. Kanwar**

**NEHA PUBLISHERS & DISTRIBUTORS**
DELHI

Publisher
NEHA PUBLISHERS & DISTRIBUTORS
4832/24 Prahlad Lane,S-207 Ansari Road,
Daryaganj, Delhi-110002 Ph: 43570876, 23278261
Email: [illegible]

Edition: 2015



ISBN : 978-93-80318-55-4

Laser Typesetting
JEE-VEE Graphics Delhi

Price : 695.00

Printed by
Vikas Computers

# CONTENTS

# SALES MANAGEMENT

## Meaning, scope, functions

## INTRODUCTION

*"Confidence and enthusiasm are the greatest sales producers in any kind of economy."*

**-O. B. Smith**

In daily life, a layman deals with different transaction in terms of selling and purchasing of goods and services. In these transactions the second one persuades the first person. Therefore, selling may be defined as persuading people to satisfy the want of first one. The person, who does this act, is called as the salesman, the result of this action as sales, while these activities of the person, are supervised and controlled by sales-management. In the present scenario sales executives are professionals. They plan, build and maintain effective organizations and design and utilize efficient control procedures. The professionals approach requires thorough analysis, market-efficient qualitative and quantitative personal-selling strategy. It calls for skilful application of organizational principles to the conduct of sales operations.

The professional approach demands the ability to install, operate, and use control procedures appropriate to the firm's situation and its objectives. Executives capable of applying the professional approach to sales management are in high demand today. The quality of selling is referred to as salesmanship. In other words, 'management' is synonymous with leadership. Managers do the same thing in industry, as ministers do in states and at the centre, i.e., they have to plan, forecast, direct and control their personnel. Here success lies in running together, hand in hand. Managers are the captains of the army of their followers.

## DEFINITION

Originally, the term 'sales management' referred to the direction of sales force personnel. But, it has gained a significant position in the today's world. Now, the sales management meant management of all Marketing activities, including advertising, sales promotion, marketing research, physical distribution, pricing, and product merchandising. The American marketers association (AMA's) definition, takes intoconsideration a number of these viewpoints. Its definitions runs like: the Planning, direction, and control of the personnel, selling activities of a business unit including recruiting, selecting, training, assigning, rating, supervising, paying, motivating, as all these tasks apply to the personnel Sales-force.

Further, it may be quoted: it is a socio-scientific process, involving' group-effort' in the pursuit of common goals or objectives, which are predetermined. Co-ordination is its key, though, no doubt, it is a system of Authority, but the emphasis is on harmony and not conflict. Sales-management differs from other fields of management, mainly in different aspects: the selling operation of a business firm does not exist In isolation. Thus, simultaneous with the changes taking place in the business, as well as marketing-orientation, a new concept of sales management has evolved. The business, is now society-oriented, on

Human-welfare aspects. So, sales-management has to work in a broader and newer environment, in co-existence with the traditional lines. The present emphasis is now on total development of human resources.

## ELEMENTS OF SALES MANAGEMENT

There are the four basic elements of sales management, discussed below:

(1) Planning: a business cannot be taken as a chance. Every salespeople or person concerned have to see for the future, in a planned way like what must be done? And who will do it?

The plan must be based on extensive market research, and the facts must be verified at every stage. The plan should also be evaluated, after investigating the total-market, for a particular type of product. Flexibility must be provided by establishing a specialist's production line, to allow for variation in production. The plan should also be subject to continued review. The details of the plan should be discussed, with all the departmental heads, concerned, and their sub-ordinates, who bear responsibility for fulfilling their parts of the plan.

(2) Co-ordination: Co-ordination is all pervasive and permeates every function of the management-process. For example, ill planning, departmental-plans are integrated into a master. Plan, ensuring adequate co-ordination. Similarly, organizing starts by co-ordination wholly, partially inter-departmental and inter-personnel matters. Co-ordination also helps in maximum utilization of human-effort by the exercise of effective leadership, guidance, motivation, supervision, communication etc. The control-system also needs coordination. Co-ordination does not have any special techniques. Nevertheless, there are sound principles, on which to develop skills. It has a special need to help the staff, to see the total picture and co-ordinate their activities, with the rest of the team. The sales manager has to encourage direct personal-contact, within the organization, particularly where there is lateral-leadership. Harmony, and not discord, should be the guiding mantra. In addition, one has to ensure free flow of information that is selective to the objectives of the business. No personal problems, arising from business operations are to be ignored, but solved through a free exchange of ideas. This is especially true in the case of the sales-force of any organization.

(3) Controlling: the sales manager has to check regularly, that the sales activities are moving in the right direction or not. He

guides, leads, and motivates the subordinates, so as to achieve the goals planned for the business. He has to take steps to ensure that the activities of the people conform to the plans and objectives of the organization. The controlling system should be such that one can study the past, note the pitfalls and take corrective measures, so that similar problems may not occur in the future. The controller has to ensure that the set targets, budgets and schedules are attained or followed in letter and spirit. There must be procedures to bring to light the failure to attain a target. The control-system has to

(i) prepare sales and market forecasts;

(ii) Determine the level of sales-budget;

(iii) Determine the sales-quotas for each salesman;

(iv) Determine, review and select distribution-channels;

(v) Organize an efficient sales force;

(vi) Establish a system of sales-reporting;

(vii) Establish a system of statistical sales-credit;

(viii) Establish stock control system(s);

(ix) Review of performance of the sales force;

In a big organization, each salesman is assigned a territory (not so big that it cannot be adequately covered). Each salesman has a target, set for specific 'period. From the weekly and monthly sales-reports, the control system is established, that will prepare records whether a particular salesman is working efficiently or not.

(4) Motivating: Motivation is essentially a human resource concept. It aims to weld together distinctive personalities into an efficient team. For this, knowledge of human psychology is needed, as a means of understanding behavior patterns.

## OBJECTIVES OF SALES MANAGEMENT

Every business firm has certain objectives to achieve. These objectives may be very explicit and definitive, or they may be implicit or general. Although, firms have different mixes of objectives, and they do place differing emphasis, on individual ones, the typical objectives include:

## *A. Fundamental Objectives*

**Sales maximization**

Sales maximization is not an easy task. Maximization of sales implies increase in the quantity of goods sold and therefore, increases in the sales volume. For a new concern, it is to start from scratch from no new experience. Most of the newly started companies follow the leaders in the line and their competitors and have a SWOT analysis -the detailed and critical study of the strengths, weaknesses, opportunities and threats.

**Profit maximization**

One might think and say that profit maximization is not a difficult task. If sales are increased profit will automatically increase. A sound firm is not interested only in the profit mazimisation but improvement in the profitability rate. It should be noted that profit and profitability are two different concepts, though they are closely related. Profit might increase in absolute terms but might not be commensurate with the efforts put in.

**Attainment of continued growth**

This objective is of topmost importance. Sale maximization and profit maximization can be attained with comparative easy and cozy efforts. However achieving continued growth is something challenging, thrilling and rewarding. Like product, each organisation has a life cycle namely birth, growth, expansion, maturity and decline. Most of the firms struggle hard to grow and expand and reach the peak heights of performance. However once they reach te peaks of prosperity and maturity, they do not stay longer in that span of lifecycle. The intelligence lies in staying evergreen at maturing stage.

## *B. Collateral Objectives*

**Identifying market opportunities and to attain them**

Sales management is responsible for foreseeing the productive market opportunities. Sale manager is a keen observer directly and through the sale force, who are operating in the target markets. They know the market position, trends, the possible quantity, quality, rice range, time duration of delivery and other consumer expectations and aspirations. This assessment of the market situation is very significant where a sales manager is moving against current in that there is keen and cut throat competition

**Forecasting and Charting the future course of operations**

Forecasting is the tough task of prognostication. It is reading the fortune. It is the mental process of imaginative and fertile thinking and magical task of matching the business variables. It is a careful task of looking before leaping. The company might have done extremely well in the past, doing much better in the present. Simply because we have smooth gliding in the past and present , there is no cause for sleeping over the matter that in the future we will be doing equally well.

**Guiding and leading the sales people and middlemen**

Direction is one of the most important functions of an able manager. Sales manager has at his command the goods and services which are to reach his customers both actual and potential. The sales people are selected, trained and placed who are the instruments of turning the organizational goals into reality. Equally important is the role of the middlemen and dealers i.e supply chain management or distribution management is contributory.

**Participatory type of management**

Setting the goals or targets for achievement is one thing and getting it achieved is another. As a sales manager, if you set the targets of you set the targets for the entire sales force and for individuals, the sales people think that these targets are given and the salesmen are to achieve them where their skills will and capabilities are taken for granted. This is one way of getting the work done. Instead the sales manager should take the sales people into confidence and ask them to set the total targets in terms of value and quantity and also individual targets at eh same time.

Generally, objectives of sales-management have to cover various sales-functions, in an integrated manner. These objectives are to be expressed, as far as possible, in measurable and quantitative terms, and should also be realistic and achievable. The setting of objectives should not be based only on the judgment of the top-management. Rather, it should be formulated and finalized, with the involvement of the sales-force, at the grass-roots level. In addition, the process of setting of sales-objectives should begin, only after the company has conducted benchmark studies, to find out, as to where it stands in terms of product, brand and market-sales and market share trends (all in measurable terms).

## NEED AND IMPORTANCE

The sales organization is required for the following purposes:

(i) To enable the top-management, to devote to more time in policy making for the growth and expansion of business.

(ii) To divide and fix authority among the sub-ordinates so that they may shirk work.

(iii) To avoid repetition of duties and functions so that there may not be any confusion among them.

(iv) To locate responsibility of each and every employee so that they can complete the whole work in stipulated time; if not then the particular person must be responsible.

(v) To establish the sales-routine in the business unit.

(vi) To stimulate sales-effort.

(vii) To enforce proper supervision of sales-force.

(viii) Setting up a sound sales organistaion.

(ix) Sound business planning.

(x) Direction and control of sales force.

(xi) Acts as a coordinator.

(xii) Contribution towards the achievement of goals.

(xiii) Building and taking advantage of ompetitive advantage.

(xiv) Building the corporate image.

(xv) Becomes an engine of growth.

## FUNCTIONS OF SALES MANAGEMENT

Sales management is a highly functional and specialized aspect of management, it functions range from pre-sales to post-sales activities. In order to achieve basic or fundamental and collateral objectives, practically it does all the functions of general management as applied to this area of sales.

### *1. Sales Planning:*

Planning is the process of thinking before doing. It works on the basis of the statement

**"Look before you leap"**

It is intellectual thinking and imaginative jiggling of business variables. It is to do with determining the future course of action. Put in other words, we are to know where we are? where we are to go? how? when? at what cost? and why?

The sales manager is expected to have a thorough knowledge of his market, product, the consumer and his sales force. He is to be aware of corporate and sales objective and the extent and nature of resources so as to make his plan not only a promising dream but a performing reality.

### *2. Sales organizing:*

Sales' planning is the first step in the sale management. The sales plan and its projections cannot be realized unless he goes ahead with sales organization. The term organization has two distinct meanings.

As a structure, it is a network of vertical and horizontal dimensions designed to attain certain definite common goals.

As a process, it is the crucial task of creating harmonious relationship between the different parts of the enterprise.

The sales manager is to design the organizational structure or the framework that clearly defines the positions and the vertical and horizontal relations. This will help in knowing how many layers are there in the organizational structure in terms of the positions such as general sales manager, administrative sales manager, field sales manager, assistant sales manager etc.

Once the positions are known, powers, duties and responsibilities of these various positions can be determined.

### *3. Sales Directing:*

The tasks of a manager does not end once he designs a plan-A blueprint of action for future period and provides a framework for relations by defining the total task dividing it and assigning it to a subordinate based on once own caliber, ability, knowledge and experience.

Manager is a leader not boss. There is vast difference between a leader and a boss.

As a leader, the sales manager is to direct and actuate his subordinates towards the attainment of selling objectives, Directing as a function of management has 3 basic ingredients namely

a) Issuing orders and instructions for the best possible performance of the various activities so assigned.

b) Guiding, teaching, coaching and making his subordinates worthy of developing self confidence of doing their work even in his absence.

c) Supervising the subordinates to ensure that their performance confers to the standards laid down in the sales plan in the coming period.

### *4. Sales co-coordinating:*

Sales activity is the outcome of a group or a team. To convert consumer desires into goods and services and back them to sales giving satisfaction to the customers and profits of the organization. Here, there is a deliberate attempt to seek co-operation of all as he desires. It should be noted that there is a vast difference between co-operation and co-ordination.

Sales manager divides his sales department as a subsystem into further minute branches of closely related and highly specialized activities. There is need of killing conflicts, bridging the gaps, compromising over individual differences though they are the members of the same team.

### 5. Sales motivating:

Motivation of people in the organization is a constructive force and a core of management process. In fact, motivation is another side of direction and leadership. It is a psychological technique of executing policies, plans and programs through the efforts of others. It is crucial task of creating a desire and inclination of willingness to perform the job in the best possible manner.

The sales manner is to design and implant a sound remuneration plan which is attractive, rewarding sales cost, sticking the employees to the organization, timely and impartial. The other side of motivation is to build morale and motivation is the cause of employee morale. Sales motivation is known for improving employee efficiency, relieving them from tension, keeping sales force happy and instilling a human treatment.

### 6. Sales controlling:

In case the earlier functions are performed in full swing and aspired, there is no need for this control function a terminal one in the process of management. It might s happen that basic selling plan might be having some laxity, there might be some lacking in organizing, direction might b wrong, there might be conflicts in case of co-ordination and even the motivation process might be defective . Hence, to correct all these laxities, lackings, wrongs, conflicts there is a need for control.

In a nutshell, sales manager plans, organizes, directs, co-ordinates, motivates and controls the sales activities operations as a part of the total work of the organization. Here, no reference is made for staffing function for it is considered as a part of organizing. In this sense, sales management plies and performs all these functions of general management as applied to sales department.

## LIVE MARKET EXAMPLE -HUL

Hindustan Unilever Ltd is the largest and the fastest moving company in FMCG. Having it's headquarter in Mumbai, it has a clientele of more than 100 million customers.

More than 15,000 employees with 1300 managers, HUL inculcates technical analysis for forecasting on a scientific basis. The planning cycle is based on the feed form generated from the distributors. The main stay of the whole system is to plan ahead. Firstly the base level demand is calculated looking at the actual sales pattern of the past 3-4 months. The forecasting is done on the SKU basis.

Efficiency of the forecast is measured with parameters such as forecast errors. The customer services efficiency is also measured based on the feedback for the customers and also the retailers who are in direct contact with the customers.

Hindustan Unilever consists of 100 manufacturing plants, 2000 suppliers; products are distributed throughout the country through a network of 4 warehouses. Having 40 agents, 7500 whole sellers and a number of large institutional customers, HUL has a network of 7000 redistribution stockiest covering a million outlets.

HUL has taken its steps in its stride and has implemented IT powered systems in its day-to-day activities.

The objective of HUL is to make the product available at right place and right time in the most cost effective manner. Here, every salesman books orders on a palm top. All orders are fed into a central database from a central point which makes for accurate on the fly demand projection and helps avoid stockout losses.

## SMBO APPROACH

It is another approach to formulate and accomplish sales-objectives is the sales management by objectives (SMBO) technique. It is formulated combined by sales manager and sales-force (representatives). It aims to focus on (i) results, within a specified set of objectives and (ii) participative style of management.

## PROCESS OF SMBO

The operationalisation of SMBO is a process, comprising of the following steps:

(i) Setting goals jointly with the salesman: In this process the goals for sales-man and sales managers are settled simultaneously in the organization so that they can built a close coordination between them and lastly they achieve the main objective of the organisation.

(ii) Planning strategy to reach the objectives: This is the participative style of sales. Management proves to be a boon to the top-management, in the sense of the close familiarity of the salesman, with their markets. The outcome of the joint exercise would be the development of a strategy that directs the salesman to his objectives, following a plan, in the correct sequence, with the correct timing, and must be efficient, in the use of resources of time and money.

## IMPORTANCE OF SMBO

The importance of SMBO for a business firm is as follows:

(a) Directing the salesman towards the broader sales and marketing objectives of the Company;

(b) Providing abetter approach, from the view-point of the salesman; and

(c) Motivating the salesman.

## CONCLUSION

In total, Selling is the act, sales is the result of this act, while salesman is the person who does this act. So, salesmanship is the quality of act of selling. Thus, selling and salesmanship cannot be used synonymously. Salesmanship serves the dual purpose of discovering and persuading prospective buyers. By his creative faculties, a salesman has not only to sell but also establish a winning, regular and permanent relationship with his customers. A satisfied customer is just the beginning of this type of relationship, which ensures future repeat orders. Sales-management is governed by the principle of management. The four elements viz.

(i) planning,

(ii) co-ordination,

(iii) controlling, and

(iv) Motivation is very relevant, as per requirement of the special nature of the business.

Objectives are equally important for sound sales management. Generally, these are:

(i) achieving sufficient sales-volume,

(ii) providing reasonable profit, and

(iii) Experiencing continuing growth.

## REFERENCES

1. www.wikipedia.com
2. Research Paper: Alvin J Silk & Ernst T. Berndt
3. Journal: National Bureau of Economic Research
4. www.marketingguru.com
5. HBR Online
6. Survey : American marketing Association
7. Advertisement and Sales Management by Sontaki
8. Marketingfunda.com
9. Nptl.com
10. www.hul.com

# FUNDAMENTALS OF SELLING

## INTRODUCTION

Today, salesmanship, publicity and sales promotion are the three wings of any successful marketing organization. "Salesmanship" is the art of winning the hearts of consumers to dispose the firm's products and services. It is the wit act of persuasion.

Selling is an ancient art, is as old as human civilization. The term salesmanship is associated with the 20th century like other words such as television, space travel, nuclear physics, video piracy and so on. The colorful history if selling and salesmanship can b traced back through the ages when these salesmen were called traders, explorers, pioneers and the world travellers. Certain distinct stages of developments are shown below:

### *1. Salesmanship*

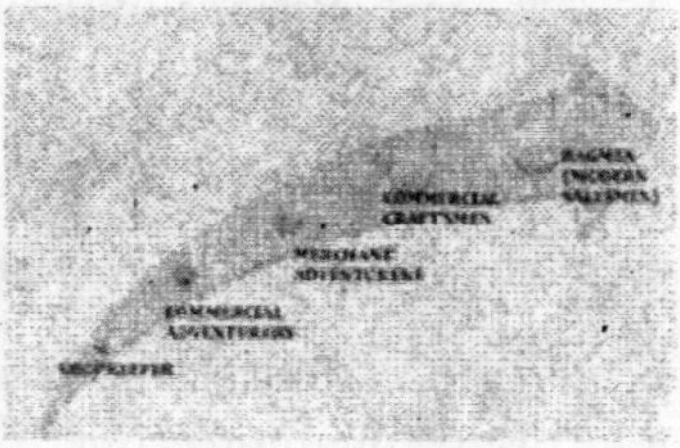

Salesmanship is the ability of a person to persuade the people to buy the goods and services for mutual gain namely, satisfaction to the buyer and profit to the seller.Some standard definition of salesmanship are given below:

*"Salesmanship consists of winning the buyers confidence for the seller's house and goods, thereby winning regular and permanent customers."*

—By Garfield Blake

*"Salesmanship is an oral presentation in a conversation with one and more prospective customers for the purpose of making sales."*

**—By American marketing association**

The efforts of salespeople have a direct impact on following areas:

- The success of new products.
- Keeping existing products on the retailer's shelf.
- Constructing manufacturing facilities. Fundamentals of salesmanship cover a detailed study about salesmen, products they sell and customers they are supposed to deal with.
- Opening businesses and keeping them open.
- Generating sales orders that result in the loading of trucks, trains, ships, airplanes, and pipelines that carry goods to customers all over the world.

### *1.1 Outstanding Attributes of Salesmanship*

- Oral Presentation
- Ability To Persuade
- Creates Customers
- Prefers "Service" To "Greed"
- Works For Mutual Gain

### *1.2 Essetials of Good Salesmanship*

- Free from exploitation
- Avoids High-haggling
- Avoids pressurization
- Believes in "customer is always right"
- Sets models for others
- Serves the customer

### *1.3 Olden and Modern Salemanship*

The art science of salesmanship as conceived, and respected today was not having the same connotation, philosophy, approach and attachment. The difference in the olden and modern salesmanship can be explained in terms of certain features, which are outlined as under:

### *1.3.1 Olden salesmanship*

**Manifestation of cheat**

In the past, salesman was most unbelievable, as they were known for fraud, dishonesty, and chicanery. The Greeks called a retailer as 'falsifier' and Roman as 'cheat'. It was true as most of the commercial adventures were pirates indulging in vessel attacks, killing the crews and seizing the cargo; they would goods to the extent of scuttling the vessels to hide their crime and traces.

**Absence of a set-price**

The good, which were dealt in did not enjoy any fixed price. It was but natural that goods were scares and the demand outstripped the supply that gave the golden opportunity to these salesmen to make hay. They did not hesitate to take full advantage of the rarity and the scarcity of the supply. The prices were unaffordable. This resulted in price high-haggling or bargaining. One tried to stretch too much. Thus, one forced encouraging another.

**Low-grade activity**

Selling, like many other ways of life, was looked down upon, as a degrading and dishonest means of livelihood. The society of these days looked at salesman with contempt and disrespect. It was because, trading itself was thought as an activity of deceit and the sellers being the party to it. The position of a salesman on a social scale was one of the lowest in terms earnings and mobility. It was considered as low grade time as the persons were to move from one place to another and person to person make their livelihood. It was true that salesman were lowest paid employees.

**Absence of publicity**

Most of the commodities were sold in small general stores. Resultantly, these were limited travelling salesman; the trading community did not rely on advertising and publicity. The methods of sale were 'sale by display' and 'sale by inspection' on the spot. Even the shops did not use attractive fixtures and furniture, artistic-decoration and painting. The concept of 'window' and 'counter' display were very crude in form.

**More an art**

Selling was taken as an art; more so a gift than acquired skill. Accordingly, good salesman were burn but not made. There was no deliberate attempt to learn the tricks of the trade; there was not such scientific training. It was not called a science and a profession as is done today. Thus, a son of a salesman would become a salesman by birth and family occupation. There was no deliberate attempt to identify it as a science and a profession. As a result, salesmanship did not flourish at the pace expected in the past.

### *1.3.2 Modern Salesmanship:*

Modern salesmanship, unlike olden salesmanship is characterized by the features of development, refinement and modernity. Today' this salesmanship is honorable, challenging, rewarding and a professional career. Today, he is not more a mule-back rider, but a ringer of door bells. Today's sales people are dynamic power in the world of business; they generate more revenue in any developed and developing economy than other workers in any other such single profession. The outstanding attributes are:

**Manifestation of commercial honesty**

Honesty is the best policy that rules the business world. Here, honesty does not mean judicial honesty. That is, each salesman is honest and truthful to the ext. He is expected to be honest. That is, he tells, demonstrates, displays, convinces by plus points of the products and services. He never blames the products of others. He says that his products are best without maligning the status of others. This approach, attitude has made the customers to behave him as a friend and a guide in making wise purchases.

**A respected profession**

Today, salesmanship is not looked only as an art and science but as a respected profession of high order. A professional professes his art and science. A profession warrants acquisition of specialized knowledge, application of knowledge as acquired, presence and respecting of a code of conduct and service to the community than self-interest, for a reasonable remuneration. Thought on the framework of these essentials and requisite salesmanship is profession challenging, rewarding, respecting and absorbing. Today, successful are professional men who have mastered the art and science of selling and sales management.

**Heavy reliance on advertising**

Today' this salesman and salesmanship rely heavily on advertising- the counterpart of product promotion mix. The sales performance of today's salesman is largely hinged on powerful force of advertising. If he is the versatile actor, advertising creates the stage and stage effects for illuminating success of his. He depends on indoor, outdoor, direct and promotional advertising media and media vehicles so much so that goods are presold. That is why advertising has been rightly described as "salesmanship in print". If one enters a shop today, it is easy to realize the deep impact of promotion publicity such as window and counter display, showrooms and show cases, fairs and exhibitions. To reach these outlets, print media, telecasting, broadcasting, film and outdoor media are a must. That is, today the work of salesman is much more easy and easy than before.

**One price policy**

With the instilled confidence and faith, the old system of bargaining is being replaced by 'one price' system. As the manufacturers and dealers announce the price of their products in advance in the advertisements and on the packages, the old system of high-haggling is fast dying. Moreover, the changed concept of 'self service' has revolutionized the marketing practices. Today, one who bargains is looked down up on; bargaining is more an act of without and represents a silly narrow mindedness in this age of affluence and plenty. The practice of 'one price' has also resulted in other guarantees and warrantees as many back speaking of honesty of purpose and action in the consumer dealings. This has resulted in saving of valuable time of both the seller and the buyer.

**Widest assortments**

The salesmanship of these days is built on the maximum consumer satisfaction. The, key to the improved consumer satisfaction is choice- variety and opportunity to select. Any dealer and his salesman is providing this facility of widest choice by making available on the counter a variety of products in a given product line. The choice is as to price, quality, size, dimensions, color combinations, aroma, weights and so on. The range of selection is so wide today that finally it is the salesman who is to help the customer in selecting a particular product.

**Sale of services**

Sale of services is another outstanding feature of modern salesmanship. A service is an intangible or impersonal activity or anticipated satisfaction that is offered for sale either as such or in connection with sale of goods.. Personal selling has upper hand in promoting the sale of services both consumer and industrial services.

## 2. PERSONAL SELLING

The personal selling is the personal communication of information to persuade a prospective customer to buy a produce or service or idea, it is the major promotional tool used to reach this goal.

The effort of sales people go far beyond simply making transactions, they also include following

- Explaining product benefits
- Demonstrating the proper operation of the product
- Educating customers about the new product
- Answering questions and responding to the objections
- Organizing and implementing point of purchase promotion.
- Arranging the terms of purchase

- Following up the purchase to ensure that customers are satisfied
- Developing the relationship with the buyers
- Collecting market and competitive information to improve marketing strategies.

## *2.1 Characteristics of Personal Selling*

Following are different features which are present in the personal seller

- Sales people represent their organization in the outside world attitudes about a company and its product are often based on the impression left by sales people
- Sales people typically operate with little or no direct supervision therefore to be successful salespeople must be creative and persistent
- Salespeople are authorized to spend company funds. they spend money for transportation, food, housing, entertainment, and other expenses
- Salespeople must frequently travel a considerable amount
- Salespeople often have profit responsibility today's salesperson do much of the strategic planning for their individual territories. In cooperation with sales manager, they decide what target market they pursue, how they will deal with each market segment.

## *2.2 Fundamentals of Successful Personal Selling*

- Sales people must have greater flexibility, he must tailor sales presentations to fit the needs and behavior of the individual customers
- He must have the potential of explaining the product benefits, answer questions of his customers
- He must be truthful
- He must behave in a reliable manner
- Must seek similarity of personality between you and the customer and the commodity interest and goals

- Sales person must see whether the person or his prospects has the potential to pay for the product or not.

## 2.3 Role of Personal Selling in Marketing

Personal selling is the interpersonal arm of promotion mix. Advertising consists of one-way, non personal communication with target consumer group in contrast personal selling involves two way personal communications between salespeople and individual consumer -weather face to face, by telephone, through videoconferences, or by other means.

## 2.4 Scope of Personal Selling

In the business there are two types of personal selling activities

- Inside selling
- Outside selling

Inside selling: It involves retail stores. In this group we include the sales person in the stores and the sales people at the catalog retailers who take telephone orders. Also included are telephone orders takes at manufactures and wholesalers, most of whom taking existing customers routine orders over the telephone. Outside selling Sales people go to the consumer. They make contact by telephone or in person. Most outside sales force usually represents producers or wholesaling, middleman, selling to the business users and not to the house hold consumers.

In outside selling, we also include:

1. Producers whose representatives sell directly to the household consumers (e.g.) insurance companies.
2. Representatives of retail organizations who go to the consumer's house to demonstrate a product, give advice, or provide an estimate such as sales people for some furniture stores and home heating and air-conditioning retailers.
3. Representative of non profitable organizations (e.g.) charity funds raisers, workers for political candidate.

## 2.5 What Makes A Good Sales Person

The term sale representative covers a broader range of positions in our economy. The position range from to the least to the most creative type of selling Sales force performs one or more of the following tasks for their companies:

- Prospecting: Sales representatives find and cultivate new customers
- Targeting: they decide how to allocate their scarce time among prospects and customer
- Communicating: sales representatives skillfully communicate information about the company's products and services
- Selling: sales person know the art of the salesmanship, approaching, presenting, answering objections, and closing sales.
- Servicing: Sales representatives provide various services to the customers - consulting on their problems rendering technical assistance, arranging financing and expediting delivery
- Information gathering: Sales representative conduct market research and intelligences work and fill in call reports
- Allocating: Sales representatives decide on which customer to allocate scarce products during product shortages

## 2.6 Principles Of Good Salemanship

Always Sell To People

- People are different ?
- No two sales are the same
- Aim at becoming a people expert
- Professional salespeople actually like people
- People buy from people - they always will?

You Have To Sell Yourself

- Be interesting ?
- Develop 'intellect' ??

- Never be arrogant - never talk 'up' or 'down' ?
- Respect the buyer and they will respect you ?
- Develop your empathy levels
- Learn to develop rapport ??
- Control your ego levels?

You Must Ask Questions And Listen To The Answers

- Develop your questioning technique
- Remember What? Where? When? Which? Why? Who? And How?
- Continually 'test your understanding'
- Listen to understand
- God has given us two ears and one mouth, we should use them in that order
- Successful sales professionals talk for 20% of the time and listen for 80% of the time
- Develop your active listening skills?

Features Must Be Linked To Benefits Remember:

- Features are common - benefits are personal and specific
- Use the 'link phrases' - 'which means that...'
- Be specific
- Sell The Results - 'Paint A Picture'
- Discover 'prime desires' ??
- Personalize benefits
- Describe end results
- You Cannot Rely On Logic
- 84% of all buying decisions are based upon emotion - not logic
- What are the chief buying emotions? - Ego - Security - Pride Of Ownership - Greed - Health - Prestige - Status - Ambition - Fear Of Loss?

Aim To Be Unique - 'Me First' Rather Than 'Me Too'

- Every business, every company, every product has something that is unique
- Look outside the square
- Identify the uniqueness of: - your product - your service - your company - yourself
- Buyers buy solutions and results they do not buy products or services?

Don't Sell On Price

- It is a 'cop out'
- Value your expertise - your products - your service and price accordingly
- Always keep the 'bottom line' firmly in your mind
- Anyone can give business away
- Selling on price means we do not need sales people?

And Finally: Be Professional At all Times

- The greatest compliment a customer can pay you is to describe you as "professional"
- Don't worry about being liked -be respected.
- Being professional is not one thing it is three:
- It is what you do, what you say and how you present yourself.

## 3. SELLING PROCESS

The selling process is essentially the series of steps followed by a salesperson through which he is offering to exchange an item of value for a different item. The original item of value being offered may be either tangible or intangible. The second item, usually money, is most often seen by the seller as being of equal or greater value than that being offered for sale.

*"Everyone lives by selling something."*

**-By Robert Louis Stevenson**

*"It used to be that people needed products to survive. Now products need people to survive."*

**-By Nicholas Johnson**

The selling process is generally divided into seven steps that, once you understand them, will empower you to sell virtually anything you want and satisfy your customers:

- Prospect and qualify
- Pre-approach
- Approach
- Presentation
- Overcome objections
- Close the sale
- Follow-up

### *3.1 Prospecting / initial contact*

Before planning a sale, a salesperson conducts research to identify the people or companies that might be interested in her product. A prospect is a lead that is qualified or determined to be ready, willing, and able to buy. New customers represent the lifeblood of a vital, growing organization.It's a key selling skill and a critical skill to develop if you want to increase your sales and achieve long-term success in sales.

### *3.2 Pre-approach*

The pre-approach is the "doing your homework" part of the process. A good salesperson researches his prospect, familiarizing himself with the customer's needs and learning all the relevant background info he can about the individual or business.It's a preparation to meet the prospect.By pre-approach, the salesman tries to make successful presentation of his goods and services before meeting the prospect.

The main objectives of pre-approach are:

- To provide additional information
- To select the best approach to meet the prospects
- To avoid serious mistakes

- To gain confidence and enthusiasm
- To save time and energy
- To be successful in the sales-interview

### *3.3 Approach*

First impressions (e.g., the first few minutes of a sales call) are crucial to building the client's trust.This usually involves introductions, making some small talk, asking a few warm-up questions, and generally explaining who you are and whom you represent. This is called the approach.Approach means meeting of the salesman and prospect in PERSON.

Thus approach aims:

- To gain favorable attention from the prospect so that he is interested enough to see the salesman.
- Securing the willingness of the prospect.

### *3.4 Presentation*

The presentation should be tailored to the customer, explaining how the product meets that person or company's needs.It might involve a product demonstration, videos, PowerPoint presentations, or letting the customer actually look at or interact with the product.

*"Nobody counts the number of ads you run; they just remember the impression you make"*

-By William Bernbach

### *3.5 Handling Objections*

After you've made your sales presentation, it's natural for your customer to have some hesitations or concerns called objections. Good salespeople look at objections as opportunities to further understand and respond to customers' needs.

The prospect can object due to following reasons:

- Fear of wrong decision
- No enough information

- No recognition of needs
- Didn't understand explanation
- Need reassurance

Three basic steps to handle objections can be as follows:

- Listen: Be attentive, maintain eye contact, and let the customer talk.
- Acknowledge: salesperson must acknowledge objections as valid but should offset them with other features and benefits.
- Restate:Brings the objection back to the customer as a selling point. When using this method, be careful not to sound as if you are trying to outwit the customer. Use a friendly, helpful tone.

## *3.6 Closing the Sale*

Closing is the art of gaining of commitment. It's needed to obtain the commitment to open the possibility of working together, which is the first and most critical commitment the salesperson must obtain. Eventually, if your customer is convinced your product will meet her needs, you close by agreeing on the terms of the sale and finishing up the transaction.Sometimes a salesperson has to make several trial closes during a sales call, addressing further objections before the customer is ready to buy.

*"You don't close a sale, you open a relationship if you want to build a long-term, successful enterprise."*

**-Patricia Fripp**

## *3.7 Following Up*

The follow-up is an important part of assuring customer satisfaction, retaining customers and prospecting for new customers. This might mean sending a thank-you note, calling the customer to make sure a product was received in satisfactory condition, or checking in to make sure a service is meeting the customer's expectations.

*"It is not your customer's job to remember you. It is your obligation and responsibility to make sure they don't have the chance to forget you."*

-Patricia Fripp

## REFERENCES


1) WEBSITES

- hhttp://www.udel.edu/alex/chapt20.html
- http://www.scribd.com/doc/6775722/Salesmanship-DBA-II-Complete-Notes
- http://www.slideshare.net/Salah35/effective-selling-process-presentation-28444073?from_search=7
- http://www.slideshare.net/shantanubera/presentation-on-selling-process?from_search=8

2) BOOKS

- Sales Management, By C.L. Tyagi, Arun Kumar
- Advertising and sales management by Sontakki

# SALES PLANNING

## INTRODUCTION

Sales planning include a set of activities that needs to be performed to achieve the goals or objectives of the sales force. It is the duty of the sales manager to create a plan that is well documented and which ensures proper management oflogistics, finance, manpower, inventories and purchases. Sales planning document is the single most important document which ensures a proper direction on how to handle the sales functions.

## ELEMENTS OF SALES PLANNING

The main elements of sales planning include the following :-

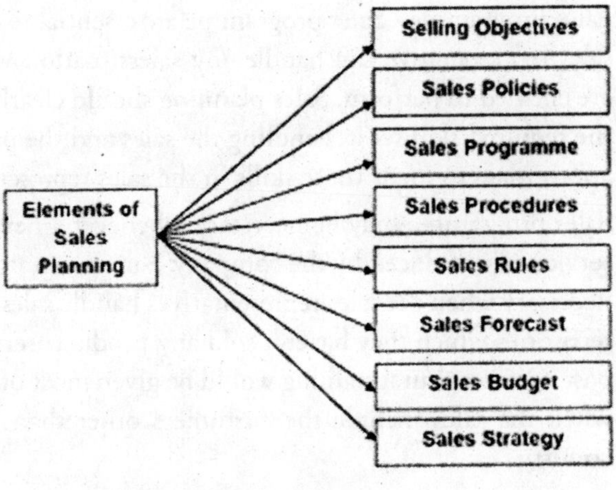

a) Selling objectives- This includes the list of objectives that need to be attained after the completion of thesales planning process. The objectives should be realistic and attainable. For example, if the sales representative is selling insurance products to the customer, a target of 20 to 30 insurance product sales per month is mostly an achievable or realistic target. If the sales planning document sets the objective as 100 insurance products, then it might not be achievable most of the times by many sales representatives. Hence the objectives must be achievable and be completed in time.

b) Sales Policies - Sales policies provide the guidelines to the sales staff to help them in performing thesales activities. Policies help the sales representatives in achieving their targets. For example, when a sale gets returned by the customer, the refund policy will guide the sales representatives how to deal with the situation effectively, so that the customer will be handled with care rather than getting into an argument. The sales policies also help in clearly identifying the right pricing for the customer depending upon the relationship the customer shares with the company. For example, if the customer is loyal to the company and is doing sales from several years, the policy would inform the sales representative about the maximum discounts that can be given to such customers.

c) Sales Programme - Sales programme are essential to ensure the sales representative can handle any salessituation which they are entitled to perform. Sales planning should clearly mention the required skill set in handling the sales and the programme appropriate to incur those skills in the sales representative.

   Sales programme may be necessary whenever a new product/ service is introduced by the company. Sales programme is also necessary when the sales representatives handle sales from new territories which they haven't sold any product/ service in the past. Cross-cultural training would be given most of the times, when the sales include the customers other than the native country.

d) Sales Procedures - Sales procedure is the sequence of various activities that need to be performed fordifferent sales functions. The sales procedures vary from sales to sale and from market to market. Sales procedure for a business to consumer sales varies greatly from business to business sales. The sales procedure may include meeting the customer, explaining the product / service through slides, use closing techniques, take the order and following up.

e) Sales Rules - Sales rules indicate the set of actions that need to be performed and not performeddepending upon the situation. For example, in credit card payments, if the customer isasking for the refund of the late payment fee, then the rule says clearly not to refund ifthe amount is received after the due date. Hence, the sales staff is not permitted torefund the amount no matter how loyal the customer is with the company.

f) Sales Forecast - Sales forecast lays the foundation of sales planning and objective setting. Based on thesales forecast the sales manager would know the sales that could be attainable for thecoming period (next quarter or year). Various time series analysis tools such as trendestimation, moving average, weighted moving average, exponential smoothing etc. may be used to forecast. Forecast can be also done based on the predictions done by the industry experts. Methods can be many but the aim of forecasting is to identify clearly the demand and plan the sales activities to generate more leads to the business.

g) Sales Budget - Sales budget identifies the necessary expenditure that is occurred in making the sales.The sales budget estimates the revenue based on sales that would be generated and identifies the profit for the organization after subtracting the operation costs of the sales staff. The sales budget would clearly set the standards for the sales team in terms of the expenditure that is permitted to incur upon the sale.

h) Sales Strategy - Sales strategy involves how the company is going to act in the market place with theproducts/ services. The market is dynamic and competitive in nature which makes thecompanies alert all the times with their pricing and position strategies. Positioning theproduct is very important since in the past many excellent products have failed due to improper positioning.

## TYPES OF SALES PLANNING

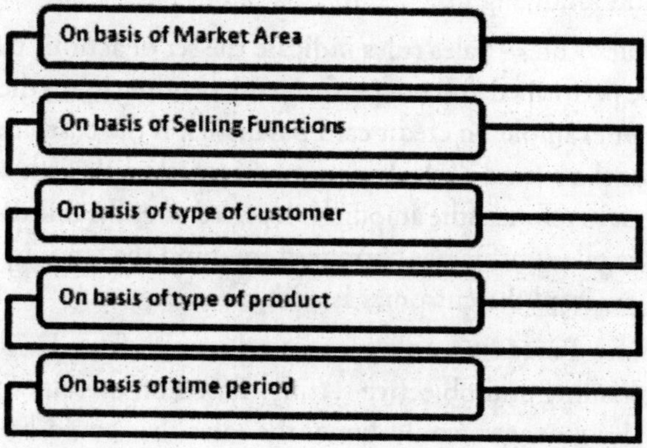


Let us look at various types of sales plans in an organization:-

a) Sales plan on the basis of market area

Whenever the sales are done in the entire country, then the entire region would be divided into several areas depending upon certain characteristics. A simple segregation would be dividing the entire country sales into different states and assigning a head for each state. For example, the in the telecommunication business, the telecom plans varies from state to state and within the state it remains the same. There are some services which are applicable for the entire country too. Even the promotional offers vary from state to state depending upon the nature of the business in these states.

Some products in FMCG sector are very strong in south and have a little presence in North and hence the companies may introduce special promotional campaigns which are available only to the northern states to improve leads. Hence the sales plan would vary from region to region.

b) Sales plan on the basis of selling functions

Sales team performs several functions such as promotions , follow up activities, presales and sales activities etc. Hence the company lays out various sales plans for each activity if necessary.

c) Sales plan based on type of customers

Most of the companies believe that 80 % of the business comes from 20 % of the key customers. Although each and every customer is important to the company, the survival of the company depends on those 20 % in difficult times. Hence following the same sales plan for all the customers wouldn't be practical since the key customer have to be handled more effectively. Hence the companies may have different sales plan for the key customers. Also the company may have different sales plan for customer depending upon the markets like B2B or B2C.

d) Sales plan based on the type of products

Every product/ service may not have the same selling activities. Hence having different sales plan is essential to handle the sales effectively. For example, if the company produces technical products, services, FMCG goods etc. it needs to have separate sales plan for the FMCG goods and the technical products and services.

e) Sales plan based on the time period

There are different sales plan for long term and short term objectives of the company. For example, increasing the sales in the already existing territory and getting sales in new territories can't have the same sales plan. Acquiring the new territory would be a long term objective whereas increasing the sales in existing territory would be a short term objective which would be a 1 year time period. For the both, strategies would be different and the operation costs would be different. Hence having a separate sales plan would be good for both the short term and the long term objectives.

## ROLE OF SALES PLAN FOR B2B AND B2C MARKETS

### *B2B markets*

B2B markets deals with the business to business deals where the time management is a critical factor for the customer satisfaction. Since the sales process takes place for months, maintaining the progress in sales is very important. The sales staff has to stick with the timings given by the customer and ensure that all the team members are present at the right time. The sales plan would deal with customers and plan the activities. There is no standardization of activities which can be applied to several customers. Since the requirements differ from customer to customer, the B2B sale plan has to deal with a flexible plan and plan the resources accordingly.

Forecasting plays a very important role in preparing a sales plan for B2B customers. The customer health in financial terms is very important and hence the customer business trend is observed time to time. Most of the times the sales are on credit basis with timely payments in regular intervals. Monitoring the forecast of the customer business will give a clear picture of the company future sales. For example, if the company is selling product "X? to the customer who in turn sells it to the customers as an accessory in his product, and if the customer business in future sees a down trend for the product "X? then it clearly indicates that the leads in future will take a downturn. In such case the company has to use appropriate sales strategies to sustain in the market place.

### *B2C markets*

B2C markets deals with business to the customer who uses the product/ service for his/her own benefit. Sales plan in B2C market has to deal with several issues related to the warehousing, distribution channels and retail.

a) Handling warehouse effectively

The sales plan has to take care that the stock of goods are ensured at all the times to handle the demand. Hence the sales plan deals with the right forecasting of the demand and give it to the manufacturing department at regular intervals so that they have the clear picture of how much and when to product the products.

Problems may occur when the goods are produced more or less than the required quantities by the market. In case of over production, goods lie in inventories there by adding up the inventory costs. In case of low production, companies may lose the customer to their competitors if the goods are not available. Hence the sales plan has to ensure that the correct information is being supplied to the manufacturing department which meets the demand and supply effectively for the organization.

Another important activity which the sales plan has to take care is to plan the warehouse according to the tax structure. For example, in India if the product in a state is not selling well and the stock has been lying idle in the warehouse, then taking the idle stock and selling in adjacent states may incur the tax of that state. Hence double taxation may take place and the profit on the product may go down to such a level where it incur loses to the company. Hence knowing the taxation structure is very important to plan the warehouse accordingly. Having the knowledge about the no tax zones also helps in decreasing the costs.

b) Handling distribution channels

The sales plan has to ensure that the regular checks are done so that the products may not end up lying in the distribution channel i.e. with the distributors due to less demand. Sales plan has to take care that the goods are distributed in necessary quantities only and are not pushed excessively into the market when the demand is less. Excessive distribution of good may damage the relationship between the distributors and the company.

This process is very critical in case of perishable goods like fruits, vegetables etc. If they lie more time in the distribution channels then the chance of them getting sold to the end customer gets decreased. It is the task of the sales plan to ensure that proper checks are done to remove excessive stock of perishable goods from the distribution channel and store them appropriately in inventories and sell them when the demand rises.

c) Handling retail stores

The sales plan has to ensure that the sales staff visits retail outlet on monthly basis and check for the stock of goods. Products that are lying for more time means that more costs have to be incurred for the shelf space. In organized retail, the shelf space comes at a cost and in case of unorganized retail, excessive stock means the company might enter into credit situation with the retailer as he/she will not be able to pay. More credit in retail may lead to untimely payments and bad relationships.

Hence the sales plan has to deal with such situations and ensure that the stock is sold properly and any excessive stock has to be removed from the retailer place. Sales plan also has to ensure that the stocks are made available all the times in case when the demand rises. Retailer interests have to be taken care of and ensuring required supply will improve the relationships.

d) Handling the price changes

Since the tax rate may go up in developing countries in small time periods and also issue of inflation, the cost of the product needs to be increased to meet the operating costs and profit margins of the company. Hence the sales plan has to handle any such situations where the price needs to be increased. As on date the government allows 10- 15 days time to sell the old stock above the MRP. Hence necessary sales activities have to be performed to deal with the price changes in the market place.

## PROCESS OF SALES PLANNING

Sales planning process appears very simple, where one can compare it to that of operating domestic central heating system. It can be as simple as - steps starting with -> setting the objectives -> determining operations necessary to meet objectives -> organising for action -> implementing -> measuring results against standards -> re evaluating and controlling. In fact there is no one universal way of establishing an ideal selling plan; neither is the process simple in actual practice because every planning situation is unique. However conceptually, the process of sales planning can be given as under:

### 1. Business Definition

As a pre requisite to the determination of sales plans, careful consideration should be given to defining and re defining the overall role or mission of the business. This is perhaps best addressed by senior management asking and answering the question "what business are we in?" Always, the definition of the role of a business should be couched in terms of what customer needs are being served by a business rather than in terms of what products or services are being produced. For instance, the manufacturer of micro computers might define the company as being in the business of rapid problem solving. In case of an automobile industry, companies might define their business as being the provision of safe transport and superior status rather the manufacture of cars. This process of business definition is extremely important because not only does it ensure that a company thinks in terms of its customers wants and needs but also in terms of the planning process, it forms a focussing mechanism for much of what follows.

2. **Analysis of current market situation**

Business definition paves the way for analysis of the current marketing situation. The precise context of this step in the preparation of sales plan will vary form company to company, but normally the analysis will encompass the following factors:

a) Market analysis

Instances of the data and analysis required under this heading would include:

(1) Current and recent size and growth of market. In the multi product company this analysis needs to be made in total, by product or market and by geographical segment.

(2) The analysis of customer needs, attitudes and trends in purchasing behaviour.

(3) The current marketing mix.

(4) Competitor analysis, including an appraisal of current strategy, current performance, including market share analysis, their strength and weaknesses and expectations as to their future action. In addition to analysing existing competition, the much more difficult task of appraising potential new entrants should be carried out at this stage.

(5) Analysis of broad macro environmental trends - economic, demographic, technological, political and cultural, which might influence the future of the company's products.

b) Analysis of SWOT

Here management must make a realistic and objective appraisal of company strengths and weaknesses in the context of potential opportunities and threats to the future of a business stem basically form factors outside the direct control of a company and in particular from trends and changes in those factors which were touched as a part of macro environment- namely, economic, political, technology and cultural factors. It is significant to recognize that the determination of what constitutes as a opportunity or threat and indeed the appraisal of strengths and weaknesses must be carried out simultaneously. An apparent strength, for instance a reputation for quality, becomes a real strength only when it can be capitalised on in the market place.

3. **Statement of objectives.**

Based on the preceding steps the company must now determine specific objectives and goals which it wishes to achieve. These objectives, in turn, form the basis for selection of selling or marketing strategies and tactics. Generally, companies have objectives in a number of areas - financial, technological objectives and so on. We are, here more concerned primarily with selling or marketing objectives, although these must be supportive of and consistent with objectives in other areas. In addition to this element of consistency, objectives should be expressed unambiguously, preferably quantitatively and with an indication of the time span within which the objectives are planned to be achieved. The time span of planned activities often five rise to some confusion in the planning literature.

Marketing or selling plans are categorised as being short range, intermediate range and long range. It is unfortunate that confusion arises from the fact that there is no accepted definition of what constitutes the appropriate time horizon for each of these categories. What is felt to compromise long-term planning in one company say 5 to 10 years may be considered intermediate in another. It is suggested that the different planning categories are identical in concept although clearly they differ in detail. Furthermore, the different planning categories are ultimately related to each other-achieving long term objectives requires first that intermediate and short term objectives be met first.

One of the most important documents in a company, however, and which sales manager will play a key role in preparing is annual sales or marketing plan.

4. **Determining Market and Sales Potential:**

A crucial step in the development of sales plans or marketing plans is the assessment of "market" and "sales" potential followed by the preparation of a detailed sales forecast. "Market potential" is the maximum possible sales that are available for the entire industry during a stated period of time; 'Sales potential' is the maximum possible portion of that market which a company can reasonably hope to achieve under the most favourable conditions. Finally the sales forecast is the portion of the sales potential that the company estimates that it will achieve. The sales forecast is in fact. A very important step in preparing the company sales plans. Not only are the marketing and sales functions directly affected in their planning considerations by this forecast, but other departments, including production, purchasing and personnel will use the sales-forecast in their planning activities.

5. **Generating and Selecting Strategies**

Once the selling or marketing objectives are clearly defined and market potential is assessed, consideration may be given to the generation and selection of strategies. Strategies, broadly, encompass the set of approaches which the company will use to achieve its objectives. This step in the process

This step in the process is complicated by the fact that there are often many alternative ways in which each objective can be achieved.

For example, an increase in sales revenue say 15 percent can be achieved by increasing unit selling prices, increasing sales volume at the company level, increase in market share or increasing industry sales. At this stage, it is advisable, if time consuming to generate as many alternative strategies as possible. In turn, each of these strategies can be further evaluated in terms of their detailed implications for resources and in the light of the market opportunities identified earlier. Finally, each strategy should be examined against the possibility of counter strategies on the part of competitors.

From this list of alternative strategies a choice must be made with regard to the broad marketing .approach which the company considers will be the most effective in achieving objectives. This must be then translated into a strategy statement which must be communicated to and agreed with all those managers who will influence its likely degree of success or failure. Once again, the specific contents of such a strategy statement will vary between companies, but as an illustration, a strategy statement might encompass the following areas: (1) A clear statement of selling objectives (2) A description of the choice of strategies for achieving these objectives (3) An outline of the broad implications of the selected strategies with respect to the following areas namely, target market, positioning, market mix and marketing research. At this stage, the strategy statement should give a clear and concise indication of where the major selling or marketing efforts of the company will be focused.

6. **Preparing the Marketing Programme:**

The strategy statement prepared provides the necessary input for the determination of the detailed programme required to implement these strategies. The first step in the preparation of this program is the determination of the marketing mix. Detailed decisions must be made in respect of product, price, promotion and place (distribution) policies. Further, care needs to be taken to ensure that the various elements of the marketing mix are integrated. That is they work together to achieve the company objectives in the most effective manner. Now the outline plan so stated guiding decision making becomes a detailed operating plan. It is on the basis of this part of the plan that day-to-day marketing activities and tactics of the company are organized, implemented and assessed.

7. **Budgeting-A Process of Resource Allocation:**

   This is the next step which is to do with resource allocation to each element of marketing mix. In most of the companies limited resources ensure that managers from different functions and areas have to compete for these scarce resources. At this stage: it is likely much detailed discussion will take place between those responsible for each element of marketing mix. In addition, it may be found that initial marketing objectives, strategies and detailed plans for the marketing programme to achieve the forecast level of sales may be unrealistic, in the light of financial and other resource constraints. In this event, modification to the original plan may have to be made. It is worthwhile to note at this stage that it can be made of both costs and revenues and a forecast profit and loss statement prepared.

8. **Implementation and Control :**

   The procedure so far outlined has resulted in preparation of a detailed document setting out what is to be done? When will it be done? Who is responsible? And the estimated costs and revenues. The details of sales plan or marketing plan, once approved, should be communicated to everyone involved. This communication is an essential, and often neglected, aspect of marketing or sales planning. It is really surprising how many companies have elaborate sales or marketing plans which are not implemented because the key people have not been informed or have not agreed to the proposed plan.

   Last, but not the least, the plan should include an outline of the control mechanism that will be applied to plan. This should include details of major objectives and key-parameters in the measurement of the degree of success in achieving the objectives. This part of the marketing or sales plan should specify what is to be measured? How is it to be measured? And what data are required for measurements? It will also include the details of what action is to be taken in the light of deviation from the plan. This is so called contingency planning is a key feature of army planning process, recognizing as it does that plans need to be flexible in order to accommodate the possible unforeseen or unpredictable changes in the market conditions.

## SUMMARY

The sales planning process helps in achieving the salesin a profitable manner, the sales planning process consists of several elements. The selling objective deals with setting realistic and attainable objectives which the sales team would work for. Also forecasting plays a very important role in predicting the future sales and setting the realistic objectives. The sales procedures, rules and policies provide guidelines to the sales representative in handling the sales task effectively. Sales plan includes the programme which ensures that the necessary skill set is inculcated to the sales staff to handle the sales. Thus sales strategy is very important to win the market place in all times.

Thus the sales plan has to effectively manage the warehouse, distribution channels, price changes and retailer in making the sales in a profitable manner to the company.

## REFERENCES

1. MukeshTrehan, RanjuTrehan (2006), "Advertising and sales management", V.K. Enterprises, New Delhi, India
2. C.N. Sontakki (2007), "Advertising and Sales Management", Kalyani Publishers.
3. http://en.wikipedia.org/wiki/Sales_and_ operations_planning

# SALES FORECAS

## 1. INTRODUCTION

Sales forecasting is a difficult area of management. Most managers believe they are good at forecasting. However, forecasts made usually turn out to be wrong! Marketers argue about whether sales forecasting is a science or an art. The short answer is that it is a bit of both. In general terms, forecasting means "A statement made about the future". So, Sales forecasting is the estimation of sales made for the future. Sales forecast is an estimate of sales in rupees or in units for future period. A sales forecast is the prediction of sales volume that a company can estimate to achieve in specified period of time in future.

Following are some of the definitions given by different scholars:

According to American marketing Association, "Sales forecast is an estimate of sales in dollars (Rupees in India) or physical units for a specified future period".

According to Matthew, Buzzles, Lovitt, Frank, 'A sales forecast is an estimate of sales of a company's product that are expected to be achieved during a given future period, in a given place'.

### *1.1 Reasons for undertaking sales forecasts:*

Businesses are forced to look well ahead in order to plan their investments, launch new products, decide when to close or withdraw products and so on. The sales forecasting process is a critical one for most businesses. Key decisions that are derived from a sales forecast include:

- Employment levels required
- Promotional mix
- Investment in production capacity

## 2. IMPORTANCE OF SALES FORECASTING

Sales forecasting is the basis of all business activities. All the business activities may it a sales related matter, production related matter, finance, advertising, etc depend on sales forecasting. Any business firm starts its plan with sales forecasting .Sales forecasting is a self-assessment tool for a company. A sales forecast reports, graphs and analyzes the pulse of any business. It is a vital basis of a company's budget. The future direction of the company depends on sales forecasting.

The importance of Sales forecasting can be stated as follows:

1. Overstocking and under stocking of materials can be maintained by a good inventory control.
2. With the help of sales forecasting, sales opportunities can be found out on the basis of the forecast.
3. All the activities in an organization are controlled on the basis of forecasting.
4. Advertising and sales promotion expenses are based on sales forecasting.
5. Sales forecasting is also important in the field of personnel department. The number of sales persons, executives etc can be increased or decreased on the basis of sales forecasting.
6. Sales forecasting is the basis for financial Planning.
7. In the field of production, with the help of sales forecasting the producer is able to adjust his production schedules and avoid idle time which leads to efficiency.
8. Supply and demand of the products can be easily adjusted.
9. It helps in knowing when and how much to buy.
10. It helps in product mix decisions.

# 3. ROLE OF SALES FORECASTING IN MARKETING

**3.1 Functions:-**

- Companies use sales forecasting to determine the existing level of demand in the marketplace, as well as future demand for a company's products or services. Forecasting can be used to predict sales revenue at a company-wide level, as well as for individual business units or product lines.

**3.2 Significance:**

- Sales forecasts directly influence a company's marketing plan. The marketing department is responsible for how customers and prospects perceive its products and services versus its competitors, and uses the sales forecast to assess how marketing spending can channel demand and increase sales.

**3.3 Time Frame**

- It is common for a company to use data from past marketing campaigns to create its sales forecast. For example, an organization may look at the number of responses from an old television ad campaign that helped increase sales during a particular season or month.

# 4. FACTORS INFLUENCING SALES FORECASTING

Following are some of the factors that influence sales forecasting:

1. Business Conditions: The sales manger should be aware of all the business condition in a country may it economic, political or business conditions. The business conditions like population growth, government policies, fashion and style etc affect sales forecasting. The economic trends such as inflation, deflation or recession etc influence sales forecasting.
2. Changes within the firm: The conditions in the industry also influence sales forecasting. For example, shortage of raw materials, shortage of finance, etc disturb the firm's activities and thus give rise to uncertainties in sales and production.

3. Internal conditions of business Enterprise: The internal conditions like pricing policy, advertising, promotion policy, selection of distribution channel etc also affect sales forecasting.
4. Taste of consumers: Different consumers have different taste. It may be any product like wearing apparel, vehicles, furniture etc. Sales depend on the size of consumers, gender, age, population etc.
5. Period: Sales forecasting is also influenced on the basis of short run, medium run and long run forecast.

## 5. TYPES OF FORECASTING

There are two major types of forecasting, which can be broadly described as macro and micro:

Macro forecasting is concerned with forecasting markets in total. This is about determining the existing level of Market Demand and considering what will happen to market demand in the future.

Micro forecasting is concerned with detailed unit sales forecasts. This is about determining a product's market share in a particular industry and considering what will happen to that market share in the future.

The selection of which type of forecasting to use depends on several factors:

(1) The degree of accuracy required - if the decisions that are to be made on the basis of the sales forecast have high risks attached to them, then it stands to reason that the forecast should be prepared as accurately as possible. However, this involves more cost

(2) The availability of data and information - in some markets there is a wealth of available sales information (e.g. clothing retail, food retailing, holidays); in others it is hard to find reliable, up-to-date information.

(3) The time horizon - that the sales forecast is intended to cover. For example, are we forecasting next weeks' sales, or are we

trying to forecast what will happen to the overall size of the market in the next five years?

(4) The position of the products in its life cycle- For example, for products at the "introductory" stage of the product life cycle, less sales data and information may be available than for products at the "maturity" stage when time series can be a useful forecasting method.

## 6. CREATING THE SALES FORECAST FOR A PRODUCT

The steps involved in creating a sales forecast are as follows:

### *6.1. Estimate Market Demand:*

Market Demand for a product is the total volume that would be bought by a defined customer group, in a defined geographical area, in a defined time period, in a given marketing environment. This is sometimes referred to as the Market Demand Curve. For example, consider the UK Overseas Mass Market Package Holiday Industry. What is Market Demand? Using the statement above, market demand can be determined as:

**Define Customer Group:** Customers Who Buy an Air-Inclusive Package Holiday Defined.

**Geographical Area:** Customers in the UK Defined.

**Time Period:** A calendar year.

**Define Marketing Environment:** Strong consumer spending in the UK but overseas holidays affected by concerns over international terrorism.

Now, the market demand could be calculated as follows:

Number of Customers in the UK: 17.5 million per calendar year.

Average Selling Price per Holiday: £450.

Estimate of market demand: £7.9 billion (customers x average price).

## 6.2. Estimate Company Demand:

Company demand is the company's share of market demand. This can be expressed as a formula:

**Company Demand = (Market Demand) x (Company's Market Share)**

For example, taking our package holiday market example; the company demand for First Choice Holidays in this market can be calculated as follows:

First Choice Holidays Demand = £7.9 billion x 15% Market Share = £1.2 billion

A company's share of market demand depends on how its products, services, prices, brands and so on are perceived relative to the competitors. All other things being equal, the company's market share will depend on the size and effectiveness of its marketing spending relative to competitors.

## 6.3 Develop the Sales Forecast:

The Sales Forecast is the expected level of company sales based on a chosen marketing plan and an assumed marketing environment. Note that the Sales Forecast is not necessarily the same as a "sales target" or a "sales budget". A sales target (or goal) is set for the sales force as a way of defining and encouraging sales effort. Sales targets are often set some way higher than estimated sales to "stretch" the efforts of the sales force.

A sales budget is a more conservative estimate of the expected volume of sales. It is primarily used for making current purchasing, production and cash-flow decisions. Sales budgets need to take into account the risks involved in sales forecasting. They are, therefore, generally set lower than the sales forecast.

## 6.4 Obtaining information on existing market demand:

As a starting point for estimating market demand, a company needs to know the actual industry sales taking place in the market. This involves identifying its competitors and estimating their sales.

An industry trade association will often collect and publish (sometime only to members) total industry sales, although rarely listing individual company sales separately. By using this information, each company can evaluate its performance against the whole market.

This is an important piece of analysis. Say, for example, that Company A has sales that are rising at 10% per year. However, it finds out that overall industry sales are rising by 15% per year. This must mean that Company A is losing market share - its relative standing in the industry.

Another way to estimate sales is to buy reports from a marketing research firm such as AC Neilsen, Mintel etc. These are usually good sources of information for consumer markets - where retail sales can be tracked in great detail at the point of sale. Such sources are less useful in industrial markets which usually rely on distributors.

## *6.5 Estimating Future Demand*

So far we have identified how a company can determine the current position:

Current Company Demand = Current Market Demand x Current Market Share

How can future market demand and company demand be forecast?

Very few products or services lend themselves to easy forecasting. These tend to involve a product whose absolute level or trend of sales is fairly constant and where competition is either non-existent (e.g. monopolies such as public utilities) or stable (pure oligopolies). In most markets, total demand and company demand are not stable - which makes good sales forecasting a critical success factor. A common method of preparing a sales forecast has three stages:

(1) Prepare a macroeconomic forecast - what will happen to overall economic activity in the relevant economies in which a product is to be sold.

(2) Prepare an industry sales forecast - what will happen to overall sales in an industry based on the issues that influence the macroeconomic forecast;

(3) Prepare a company sales forecast - based on what management expect to happen to the company's market share

Sales forecasts can be based on three types of information:

(1) What customers say about their intentions to continue buying products in the industry.

(2) What customers are actually doing in the market.

(3) What customers have done in the past in the market.

There are many market research businesses that undertake surveys of customer intentions - and sell this information to businesses that need the data for sales forecasting purposes. The value of a customer intention survey increases when there are a relatively small number of customers, the cost of reaching them is small, and they have clear intentions. An alternative way of measuring customer intentions is to sample the opinions of the sales force or to consult industry experts

### *6.5.a. Non-Quantitative or Qualitative Techniques for Forecasting Sales*

Non-Quantitative or Qualitative forecasting techniques are sometimes referred to as judgmental of subjective techniques because they rely more upon opinion and less upon mathematics in their formulations. The absence of past sales means that you have to be more creative in coming up with prediction in the future. Sales forecast for new products are often based on executive judgments, sales force projection, surveys and user's expectation. Qualitative techniques are recommended for those situations where managers or sales force are particularly adept at predicting sales revenues. These techniques are often utilized when markets have been disturbed by strikes, wars, natural disasters, recessions or inflation. Under these conditions historical data are useless and judgmental procedures that account for the factors causing market stocks are usually more accurate.

Non Quantitative or Qualitative forecasting techniques which include:

## Non-Quantitative Techniques for Forecasting Sales

### Sales Force Composite

| | |
|---|---|
| Characteristics | o Salespeople each estimate their territory<br>o May consult supervisor<br>o Individual forecasts are combined and adjusted for each office<br>o Used by 60-70% of all companies |
| Advantages | o Salespeople know the actual sales potential in their territories<br>o Salespeople are closest to the source.<br>o Salespeople accept the forecast because they did it<br>o Put responsibility for forecasting in the hands of those that can make it happen<br>o Statistical and technical errors are minimized<br>o Detailed final forecast is done by product, customer, market<br>o Can be done with little or no data or history |
| Disadvantages | o Salespeople are not trained forecasters<br>o Salespeople focus on the present. They do not anticipate environmental change .<br>o Salespeople may be too optimistic<br>o They may go low so that they have an easier time hitting quota<br>o Takes time away from selling<br>o The salespeople may not be that interested. They could do a real sloppy job |

Application:

| | |
|---|---|
| Best used for companies | o Industrial products |
| | o Few customers |
| | o Seasoned, skilled sales people |

**Jury of Executive Opinion**

| | |
|---|---|
| Characteristics | o Opinions of a group of executives are pooled |
| | o Data may be compiled by each executive or by marketing research |
| | o Individual forecasts may be combined by a specialist or |
| | o Individual forecasts may be combined by negotiation as a group |
| | o This method is valued as most important to marketing managers |
| Advantages | o Easy, quick, not much math |
| | o Opinions from all over the firm are integrated |
| | o Usually inexpensive |
| Disadvantages | o Opinion based not data (fact) based |
| | o Takes executives away from their jobs |
| | o People with no marketing knowledge, like accountants that fail Marketing 370, are making market forecasts |
| | o Hard to break down to territories |
| | o Hard to break down for tasks |
| Application | o A small group should be used |
| | o They should be very well informed |
| | o They need access to data |
| Factor Listing | |
| A variation | o Each exec lists factors that might impact sales |

- o Positive and negative factors are separated into two groups
- o Consensus on the magnitude of the sales impact of each factor is reached
- o Each magnitude is added (subtracted) from this year's sales

Delphi Technique

A variation
- o Jury members never meet face to face
- o Comprehensive and representative jury of experts
- o Jury members make anonymous forecast
- o Leader averages and sends it back to jury members
- o Jury members then resubmit
- o Keep repeating until a consensus is reached

Survey of Buyer Intentions

Characteristics
- o Sample or census of buyers tell their buying intentions
- o Responses are added and applied to the market for a forecast

Underlying Assumptions about Customers
- o Have the ability to predict in advance
- o Have a track record of following through with their plans
- o Have the financial capacity to follow through with their plans
- o Are willing to disclose or share their plans

Advantages
- o Actual buyers make the forecast

| | |
|---|---|
| | o If there are few customers then this is fast, cheap, easy |
| | o May be the only method available for products with no history |
| Disadvantages | o Buyers don't know what they are going to do |
| | o Difference between desires and reality |
| | o Buyers may consider the information confidential |
| | o Surveys are expensive, time consuming |
| | o Derived demand, the multiplier effect may kick in |
| Application | o Use with at least one other method |
| | o Use when there are not many customers |
| | o Use when you can't use anything else |

### *6.5.b. Quantitative Techniques for Forecasting Sales*

Quantitative techniques are sometimes termed objective or mathematical techniques as they rely more upon mathematics as less upon judgment in their computation. These techniques are now very popular as a result of sophisticated computer packages. There are many quantitative techniques:

**Quantitative Techniques for Forecasting Sales**

**Trend Projections**

| | |
|---|---|
| Characteristics | o Extrapolate simple trends |
| | o Same as last year |
| | o Same percentage as last year |
| Advantages | o Easy, fast, cheap |
| | o Reliable for mature products |
| Disadvantages | o Assumes no change in the environment |
| Application | o Mature, Stable products and companies |

Fitting a Trend-Line

| | |
|---|---|
| Assumptions | o Sales influences fall into four categories |
| | • Trends (long term changes) |
| | • Cyclical changes |
| | • Seasonal changes |
| | • Irregular changes |
| Characteristics | o Uses least squares to determine slope and intercept of a straight line |
| Advantages | o Easy to get internal data |
| | o Quick and easy (use excel) |
| | o Can use a long historical period |
| Disadvantages | o Assumes no changes in the environment |
| | o Need lots of history |
| | o Can't Use for short terms |
| Application | o Stable industries |

Moving Averages

| | |
|---|---|
| Characteristics | o Short term see example |
| Advantages | o Removes seasonally |
| | o Short term changes unlikely |
| | o Good when things are stable |
| Disadvantages | o Does not respond to a rapid shift |
| | o Assumes no environmental changes |
| | o Data storage costs |
| | o Equal weighting of all the months in the series |
| Application | o short term inventory control |

Exponential Smoothing

| | |
|---|---|
| Characteristics | o another short term |
| | o See Example |

| | | |
|---|---|---|
| Advantages | o | Don't need long series |
| | o | More weight can be given to recent months |
| | o | Easy |
| Disadvantages | o | Still might not respond to a rapid shift |
| | o | Assumes no environmental changes |
| Application | o | Short term inventory control |
| Correlation-Regression | | |
| Characteristics | o | Considers causality |
| Step one | o | Determine independent variable(s) |
| Step two | o | Measure correlation |
| Step three | o | compute slope and intercept |
| | o | Obtain forecast of independent variables |
| | o | Forecast |
| Advantages | o | Can determine causality |
| | o | can account for environmental change |
| | o | May actually develop leading indicators |
| Disadvantages | o | dependent on forecast of independent variables |
| | o | Can be time consuming, expensive and get sophisticated in a hurry |
| | o | Can make you forget to look at the real world |
| Application | o | Longer term forecasts |
| Econometric Models | | |
| Characteristics | o | Two or more independent and dependent variables |
| | o | Forecast of one dependent variable might influence other variables |
| | o | Follow the same steps |

Advantages
- o Tight relationships and interrelationships uncovered
- o Major changes can be anticipated
- o Can be used as a model for simulation

Disadvantages
- o Expensive, require experts
- o Must be continually monitored
- o Lots of data needed
- o Data quality must be verified

Application
- o Long term
- o industry or larger firm

Objective versus Subjective Analysis
- o quantitative techniques reduce guesswork
- o They don't do it all

The Limitations of Forecasting
- o A good sales forecast cost money
- o Sales forecasters seldom have all the time they deem necessary
- o Sales forecasts are estimates
- o Changes in fundamental conditions can cause the forecast to vary from actual results

Modern Managers have several different methods available for Sales Forecasting. Popular methods are:

- Jury of Executive Opinion Method: In the Jury of executive opinion method of Sales Forecasting, appropriate managers within the organization assemble to discuss their opinions on what will happen to sales in the future. Since these discussion sessions usually resolve around hunches or experienced guesses, the resulting forecast is a blend of informed opinions. A similar, forecasting method, which has been developed recently is called the DELPHI Method. Delphi Method also gathers, evaluates, and summarizes expert opinions as the basis for a forecast, but the procedure is more formal than that for the jury of executive opinion method.

The Delphi Method has the following steps:

1. STEP 1 - Various Experts are asked to answer, independently and in writing, a series of questions about the future of sales or whatever other area is being forecasted.
2. STEP 2 - A summary of all the answers is then prepared. No expert knows, how any other expert answered the questions.
3. STEP 3 - Copies of summary are given to the individual experts with the request that they modify their original answers if they think it necessary.
4. STEP 4 - Another summary is made of these modifications, and copies again are distributed to the experts. This time,however, expert opinions that deviate significantly from the norm must be justified in writing.
5. STEP 5 - A third summary is made of the opinions and justifications, and copies are once again distributed to the experts. Justification in writing for all answers is now required.
6. STEP 6 - The forecast is generated from all of the opinions and justifications that arise from step 5.

- The Sales force Estimation Method: The Sales Force Method is a sales forecasting technique that predicts future sales by analyzing the opinions of sales people as a group. Sales people continually interact with customers, and from this interaction they usually develop a knack for predicting future sales. As with the jury of executive opinion method, the resulting forecast normally is a blend of the informed views of the group. The sales force estimation method is considered very valuable management tool and is commonly used in business and industry throughout the world. This method can be further improved by providing sales people with sufficient time to forecast and offering incentives for accurate forecasts.

Companies can make their sales people better forecasters, by training them to better interpret their interactions with the customers.

- Time Series Analysis Method: Many businesses prepare their sales forecast on the basis of past sales. Time series analysis involves breaking past sales down into four components:

(1) The trend: are sales growing, "flat-lining" or in decline?

(2) Seasonal or cyclical factors. Sales are affected by swings in general economic activity (e.g. increases in the disposable income of consumers may lead to increase in sales for products in a particular industry). Seasonal and cyclical factors occur in a regular pattern;

(3) Erratic events; these include strikes, fashion fads, war scares and other disturbances to the market which need to be isolated from past sales data in order to be able to identify the more normal pattern of sales

(4) Responses: the results of particular measures that have been taken to increase sales (e.g. a major new advertising campaign)

Using time series analysis to prepare an effective sales forecast requires management to:

- Smooth out the erratic factors (e.g. by using a moving average)
- Adjust for seasonal variation
- Identify and estimate the effect of specific marketing responses

## 7. CONCLUSION

One of the keys to success in sales is knowing where are customers are located and being able to predict how much they will buy. Sales forecasting is so important that more then 50% of companies include this topic in their sales manager training programs. Inaccurate demand predictions can have disastrous effects of profitability. Managers should calculate and record the forecasting errors produced by the qualitative techniques they employ so that will know when these methods are best employed. Qualitative techniques are often used in conjunction with the quantitative techniques.

Most initial sales forecast today are prepared with computer program. A recent survey of 207 firms revealed that 76% of the companies allowed managers to make adjustments to computer generated forecast with judgmental procedures. Quantitative forecasting techniques are best employed when companies have access to historical data. Quantitative techniques have distinct advantages in situations where managers must make frequent forecasts for hundreds or thousands of products.

Because of the large number of calculation required by quantitative forecasting procedures, analysts need access to computers and appropriate forecasting software. The successful use of quantitative technique demands that analysts be well versed in the statistical procedures used by these techniques.

## 8. REFERENCES


1. Dalrymmpple, Cron, DeCarlo, 2004, Sales management, Hoboken, Wiley, Eight edition, p94.
2. Futrell Charles M. , Sales Management -Teamwork, Leadership and Technology, Orlando, The Dryden Press, 1998., p.167
3. Jobber, D. and Lancaster, G., Selling and Sales Management, London, Pearson Education, (2003), p. 412-3.
4. Mentzer J., Kahn K., Forecasting Techniques Familiarity, Satisfaction, Usage and Application, Journal of Forecasting, Vol 14., John Wiley&Sons, 1995., p. 465-476.
5. Vukovi? Ph D Nahod, Forecasting, Lecture, Faculty of Organizational Sciences, University of Belgrade, 2006.
6. http://www.benchmarkingreports.com/salesand marketing/ sm_ 115_sfa_profiles.asp0

# SALES TERRITORIES AND QUATOS

## SALES TERRITORIES

A sales territory is the customer group or geographic district for which an individual salesperson or sales team holds responsibility. Territories can be defined on the basis of geography, sales potential, history, or a combination of factors. Companies strive to balance their territories because this can reduce costs and increase sales.

## REASONS TO DESIGN SALE TERRITORIES

When you originally designed your sales territories, you are attempting to do 3 things:

1. Organize the workload across territories in order to allow for equal coverage and representation of existing customers and prospects
2. Balance territory revenue potential across territories to allow for even rewards and incentives to all sales reps
3. Economize and Increase Efficiency of your sales force overall, whether by reducing travel time or increasing vertical industry expertise

### Do I Need to Redesign My Sales Territories?

Consult our list to determine if you need to make some changes to your sales territories:

1. Change in the Size of the Sales Force (expansion or contraction) - A sales force of 8 sales reps will undoubtedly split up a territory

differently than a sales force of 18. As your organization's staff size changes, you must take into account the effect it has on your sales territories.

2. Change in the Products or Services Offered - If your organization launches a new product or service, this can have huge effects on the alignment and balance of your sales territories. What happens if one territory has a greater demand for this new product? All of a sudden that territory needs more representation from your sales force. You also may need to shuffle your sales reps around depending on product expertise.
3. Changes to Client Classification - You don't only have to make sales territory alterations to accommodate your own organization. You may have to perform a redesign to account for client changes as well. In the present-day business world, organizations are always shifting.
4. Supporting Sales Rep Career Progression - As sales reps grow in their respective careers, and advance through your organization, they will naturally shift into different positions. The original reason that you designed a sales territory around a strong regional rep in a major metro area is bound to change when he/she becomes a national rep.
5. Making Accommodations for Sales Rep Requests - Sales reps will often make specific requests concerning their sales territories. Examples may be along the lines of, "I live closer to this territory," or "I drive through this territory every day," or "I have stronger connections in this territory."

## BENEFITS OF SALE TERRITORIES

- Increase sales potential - improved customer coverage allows your sales force to spend more time in front of customers and prospects and less time traveling
- Decrease cost of sales - Optimally aligned territories result in shorter drive times and associated travel expenses for sales people, making each sale more profitable

- Gain competitive advantage - With optimally aligned territories, you can move faster when new opportunity comes in, beating your competition to the next sale
- Improve sales force satisfaction - Balanced workloads and earning potential will improve morale and career satisfaction among your sales force, leading to higher motivation and lower turnover

## PROCEDURE FOR DESIGNING SALES TERRITORIES

Start the territory design process by looking at your entire market.. Your entire territory. If you have five salespeople that cover it for you. Then you would have a minimum of five territories within your market. When you do your territory planning, look to the future. If you're thinking of adding two salespeople. Add those sales territories now while you are going through this territory planning process? The two new territories can be worked by the existing salespeople until the new salespeople are hired.

- Start By Looking At Your Base

  To get this territory planning, done right, Start with your existing customer base. I like to get a picture of where my entire customers' base is located. If your organization has market segments, this is a good time to look at each of those segments individually.
- Look At Revenue by Account

  The second step in territory planing is to look at the revenue for each of your clients. Then take a look at their future sales potential.
- Are Prospects Or Market Potential Evenly Distributed?

  Let's say your ideal prospect is a company in the construction industry. Construction companies that do interiors for the commercial office buildings. How many of them are there in your market? Where are they located?
- Decide basic territories by build up method

## PROCEDURE IN BUILD UP METHOD

The breakdown method is the reverse of the buildup method and in this, the market potential for the product is identified and then the market share that the company is targeting assessed. Based on this, sales are forecast. This is followed by determining the average number of sales that each salesperson is required to make and the territories are then accordingly allocated to individual salespersons. In the incremental method, additional territories are created as long as the revenues generated from them exceed the cost of serving them.

## ASSIGNING SALES PERSON TO A TERRITORY

### Basic qualities required in salesperson

### Prospecting

Without a consistently full pipeline, you will struggle to meet your sales targets and goals. You will experience peaks and valleys and experience a great deal of frustration. Unfortunately, very few companies actually teach sales people how to prospect effectively. And the vast majority of sales people rely on just a few prospecting methods such as cold calling or networking.

### Questioning

Although this sounds like a fundamental concept, the majority of sales people I have encountered over the last 15 years fail to effectively execute it.

Many sales people ask low-value questions that do little to engage their prospects in the sales conversation. Examples include:

"Are you the decision maker?"

"What's your budget?"

Unfortunately, too many sales people still ask tired, out-dated questions like these. As a result, they fail to differentiate themselves from the competition or demonstrate their expertise.

True sales professionals know how to ask high-value questions. Questions that encourage their prospect to share details and information about their business that, in turn, will help the rep effectively position their solution. Questions like:

"What goals are you striving to achieve this quarter?"

"What challenges are you experiencing trying to reach those targets?"

"What are those problems costing you in terms of lost revenue, customers, market share, etc.?"

"What impact is that having on your business?

**Listening**

You can ask all the questions in the world but if you don't listen carefully to what the other person tells you, you are wasting your time and losing valuable sales opportunities. True listening means that you stop multi-tasking during a telephone conversation. Don't type notes into your computer, scan emails or anything else.

**Presentation Skills**

Two aspects of presentations need to be considered:

A. The content. Too many sales people include far too much information in their presentations and open them by talking about their company instead of the buyer's situation. Resist the "include everything but the kitchen sink" approach and only discuss the aspects of your offering that are critical for your prospect to know.

B. The verbal presentation. Consider your pace, timing and actual delivery. The more important a potential sale is for you, the more critical it is that you verbally rehearse that presentation. Watch your body language, gestures, and facial expressions.

The best way to improve your presentation skills is to videotape a presentation and watch it afterwards.

**Rapport-building**

Developing a connection is still important in today's sales environment even though we rely heavily on technology. People still buy from people. Creating rapport with someone means connecting with them. This does not mean that you talk about a photo on the desk or an award on their wall...that approach is severely outdated. Instead, you need to be able to speak your prospect's language. You need to demonstrate that you understand the business problem they face.

**Objection handling**

Objections are a natural part of the sales process. However, how you respond to them can make or break a deal.However, before you respond follow these three short steps first.

1. Empathize. This means verbally stating that you understand, respect or appreciate the other person's concern. "Mr. Smith, I understand that you have budget issues to deal with."
2. Clarify. Restate the objection back to the prospect in your own words to ensure that you clearly understand it "So you see the value in this product, it's just that the purchase exceeds the budget you had allotted, correct?"
3. Seek permission. Ask the other person for permission to offer a solution. "Mr. Smith, would it be okay if I took a minute to discuss a few options?"

**Persistence**

If you want to achieve long-term success in sales you MUST be persistent. However, there is a significant difference between being persistent and stalking someone. Persistence means finding creative ways to keep your name in your prospect's mind. Persistence means not allowing the first few no's to prevent you from pursuing high-value, legitimate sales opportunities.

**Organizational Skills**

To succeed in sales you need a plan. You need to be organized. You need to be able to outline your day, week and monthly schedule in order of priority. You need to juggle the demands placed on your time because it is virtually impossible to get everything done that you need to in a given day.

**Focus**

Lastly, sales people need to have focus. There are a multitude of distractions that threaten to challenge your focus. Email, telephone calls, text messages, problems, paperwork, and traffic are just a few.

Being able to maintain your focus on the big picture as well as the smaller details can make the difference between success and failure.

## MANAGEMENT OF TERRITORIAL COVERAGE

How sale person is going to cover the area .

It requires 3 basic steps to be followed

1) Planning efficient route for sale person
2) Scheduling sale person `time
3) Using time management tools

ROUTING

Routing is the process of moving packets across a network from one host to a another. It is usually performed by dedicated devices called routers.

Packets are the fundamental unit of information transport in all modern computer networks, and increasingly in other communications networks as well. They are transmitted over packet switched networks, which are networks on which each message (i.e., data that is transmitted) is cut up into a set of small segments prior to transmission. Each packet is then transmitted individually and can follow the same path or a different path to the common destination. Once all of the packets have arrived at the destination, they are automatically reassembled to recreate the original message.

## ROUTING GUIDELINES

Following these guidelines will help in ensuring that tours are as short as possible:

- tours should be circular
- tours should not cross
- the same route should not be used to go to and from a customer
- customers in neighboring areas should be visited in sequence

## ROUTING PATTRENS

More efficient (shorter) routes will tend to exhibit one of these patterns:

- hopscotch

- cloverleaf

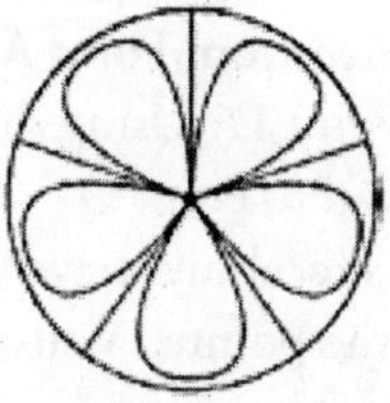

Note that the cloverleaf pattern better follows the guidelines that were given above. Indeed, with the example territories and focal point above, the cloverleaf routes would probably require less travel time if such routing is possible on existing roads.

The above circular area was divided into five equally sized territories with a focal point at the center. A route to visit customers in the territories was then drawn in either a circular clover leaf pattern or in a hopscotch pattern. This way of making territories and of routing sales calls would be appropriate if, say, five salespeople reported to a common office in the center. It would also be appropriate if, say, a single salesperson was assigned to a remote territory and must divide the territory into five daily routes to visit customers once per week.

## THE TRAVELING SALESPERSON PROBLEM: HEURISTICS FOR DEVELOPING EFFICIENT ROUTES

It would seem that there should be some sort of mathematical method for developing the shortest tours within a territory, but there is no way to develop the shortest route other than to try every combination or roads possible. If the routes are constantly changing - as when a salesperson has a different set of prospects to visit every day - then this is not feasible. Fortunately, there are some heuristics that can be used to find routes that tend to be reasonably short.

## Largest Angle Heuristic

Consider the choice below:

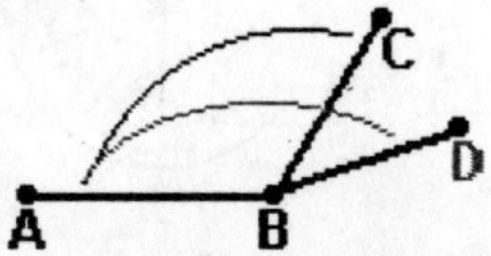


You have traveled from Point A to Point B. Should you travel next to Point C or Point D? Using the Largest Angle Heuristic, you should choose to travel to Point D. When choosing a route using the Largest Angle Heuristic, always travel next to a point which generates the largest angle to the pointed visited last.

This heuristic will help to ensure that the route is circular and tends to generate efficient routes.

## Closest Next Heuristic

Consider the choice below:

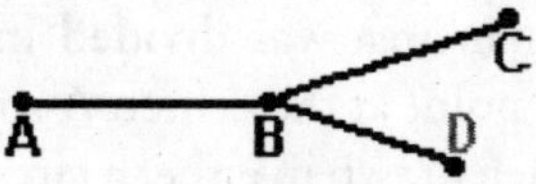


You have traveled from Point A to Point B. Should you travel next to Point C or Point D? Using the Closest Next Heuristic, you should choose to travel to Point D. When choosing a route using the Closest Next Heuristic, always travel next to a point which is closest to where you are right now.

This heuristic also tends to generate efficient routes. Which is better, the Largest Angle Heuristic or the Closest Next Heuristic? There is no good answer to this question; the only way to find the optimal route to a particular problem is to simulate every possible route on a computer (or by hand) - a very time consuming process. A realistic problem for a salesperson is to generate a reasonably good route for a single day. Using these heuristics, you might not always find the optimal route, but you can quickly rough out a route that generally is relatively good with very little investment in time.

In using these heuristics to make decisions, you should also use the Look Ahead procedure. That is, don't simply look at the next point in a route, but look ahead two points and use try both of the above heuristics to make a decision for the next two points.

## TIME MANAGEMENT

The art of managing time is based on a few simple and proven techniques. Only with practice can it become an ingrained habit that can produce amazing sales results.

- o Get Organized: Getting organized is the first step towards managing time effectively. Highly successful sales people have their calendars chalked out for a year in advance.
- o Visualize your action plan for the full day. Do it after the morning work out or the previous evening
- o Delegate tasks to others to save time. responsibilities of completing a task as well as earning something extra.
- o Do not procrastinate. It is the biggest time stealer. Finish off things as and when scheduled.
- o Some sales executives take up the easy jobs first and keep the most difficult ones towards the end. Tackle the difficult tasks first.
- o Staying clear of negative thoughts and negative people is a huge time saver.
- o Use your down or wait times creatively. As a sales professional, you probably spend a lot of time in your car in traffic getting to your next appointment.
- o The above time saving tips are based more on common sense. There are other time saving and productivity enhancing tips that are backed by solid research as well.
- o Analysis of revenue growth curves of successful sales professionals reveal that it's not important how much total time they spend on sales activities rather than how they allot their time.

- o The survey also establishes that high sales performers spend less time on administrative work - 30% less than the low performers.

## SALES QUATAS:- MEANING AND DEFINATION

A quota, or sales goal, is a set amount of selling that a salesperson is expected to meet over a given time frame. Nearly all companies set quotas for their salespeople, as a quota both ensures that a salesperson knows what is expected of him and is the easiest way to determine what commissions are due for that salesperson.

While quotas are widespread in the sales industry, the form they take can vary considerably from company to company. A small business with a handful of salespeople and one or two products to sell will probably set a very simple quota - for example, the goal might be for each salesperson to sell $100,000 worth of products per calendar quarter. On the other hand, a large company with thousands of sales reps and many different products or services may set a very complex quota consisting of different targets for different products - 100 units of product A, 50 units of service B, $1,000 worth of add-on services such as warranties, and so on. In the case of a large company with offices spread out over a wide geographic area, goals for each office will probably differ based on their perceived potential.

Quotas may be set for time periods ranging from weekly to yearly, but quarterly quotas are probably the most common. A quarterly period gives salespeople plenty of time to align their sales strategies to their goals and set a sales plan in motion. Quarterly quotas also help companies take product seasonality into consideration. If a particular product sells much better in summer than in winter, then the company can have a higher quota in Q3 than it does in Q4 and make more revenue without putting too much strain on the sales team.

## METHODS FOR SETTING SALES QUATAS

Setting quotas for a sales staff works in two different ways. First, your employees will have a set goal that they have to meet and that works as a powerful motivator. Second, you can better weed out salespeople who may not be as talented or able to meet their quotas on time. It is important to set fair quotas that will motivate your team without being impossible to attain.

**Step 1**

Work with your sales team to develop quotas. Your sales staff has a good idea of what the market will bear and what they are able to produce. Instead of just producing an arbitrary figure and expecting them to meet it, it is important to discuss sales quotas with them and find a figure that both parties can agree upon and meet.

**Step 2**

Consider how much you would like your business to grow. One good rule of thumb in setting sales quotas is to take last year's sales numbers and add 10 percent. This is a solid indicator of growth and is not unattainable.

**Step 3**

Add up how much revenue you expect your sales team to bring in. When you know how many sales you need to make a profit, this can help you develop a quota.

**Step 4**

Stair-step quotas. You may have sales people who are incredibly talented and can handle larger quotas. On the same token, you may have new sales people that have not quite found their stride yet. Assign larger quotas to team members who are capable of meeting those goals.

**Step 5**

Pay attention to market conditions. If your local economy is going through a depression or recession, you need to pay attention to this information. Sales will likely be lower until the economy rebounds.

## WHY SETTING QUATA IS A CHALLENGE ?

Sales leaders want to achieve their sales goals. After all, that's job #1. But what is their #1 challenge? According to a recent Alexander Group survey, 61% of sales leaders say it is setting quotas. Surprisingly, most sales leaders spend very little time devoted to this exercise.. However, careful analysis of previous quota performance distributions can yield a wide range of findings and insights. Not only does it shed light on what future distributions may look like, but it may also shed light on a variety of sales force issues. A normal, bell-shaped quota distribution is critical to maintaining a well-motivated and cost effective sales force

**Why Is Quota Setting Such a Challenge?**

And what causes skewed attainment distributions? Here are some of the prevalent reasons:

- Top-down corporate approach with little to no bottom-up sales force collaboration
- Peanut butter approach: "Let's take last year's performance, add 10% across the territories"
- Procrastination: late process results in a rush job and quotas released well after the new year begins
- Over-allocations driven by unrealistic corporate expectations
- Complex sales crediting rules (rampant double crediting)
- Emotions: fear of losing talent leads to favoritism to top performers
- Poor insight into market potential, etc.

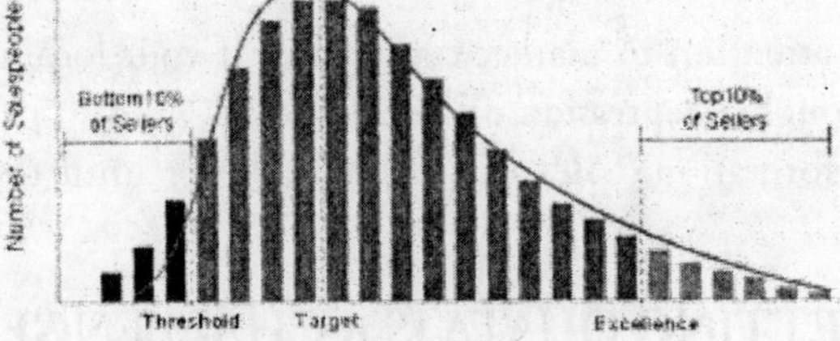

**What is a "good" quota distribution?**

Quota distributions should be a balanced and normally distributed mix of sales rep winners (those who achieved some level of outstanding pay beyond 100% of goal) and those who are less than 100% of goal. Typically ~60% of reps should achieve 100% of their goal or greater, and ~40% will achieve less than goal. See below. Sales organizations should strive for consistently achieving this balance globally, within geographic regions, within job roles and on an annual basis.

**A Fact-Based Approach.**

Quota programs and the forecast processes that global and regional personnel follow year over year don't typically change, causing attainments to become more and more skewed over time. Good quota programs involve three things: 1) an appropriate quota methodology (such as modified fair-share), 2) a well-defined process (such as a combined bottom-up, top-down approach), and 3) a tool or system that can effectively track and manage quotas.

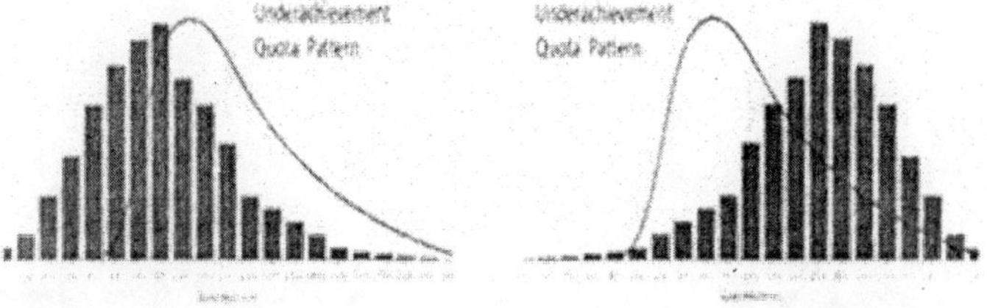

Digging Deeper. Skewed attainment curves, or worse, a bi-modal curve, could indicate issues beyond quota setting. Complete quota program assessments involve deeper review of sales performance, sales process analytics, role clarity, account targeting, and compensation and crediting rules, among other things. Root causes of recurring skewed patterns of attainment can be rectified.

## CONCLUSION

So at the end we can say that sale territories should ve properly designed and quoata must be properly set according to the capabilities of sale person. Proper person should be assigned as a sales person and proper training should be given.more territorial coverage as possible should be managed so that more area can be covered. Proper method should be used in designing territories and time management tools should be used. Problems of the sales person should be properly solved.

# SALES BUDGET

## SALES BUDGET: DEFINITION AND EXPLANATION

A sales budget is a detailed schedule showing the expected sales for the budget period; typically, it is expressed in both dollars and units of production. An accurate sales budget is the key to the entire budgeting in some way. If the sales budget is sloppily done then the rest of the budgeting process is largely a waste of time.

The sales budget will help determine how many units will have to be produced. Thus, the production budget is prepared after the sales budget. The production budget in turn is used to determine the budgets for manufacturing costs including the direct materials budget, the direct labor budget, and the manufacturing overhead budget. These budgets are then combined with data from the sales budget and the selling and administrative expenses budget to determine the cash budget. In essence, the sales budget triggers a chain reaction that leads to the development of the other budgets. The selling and administrative expenses budget is both dependent on and a determinant of the sales budget. This reciprocal relationship arises because sales will in part be determined by the funds committed for advertising and sales promotion.

The sales budget is the starting point in preparing the master budget. All other items in the master budget including production, purchase, inventories, and expenses, depend on it in some way. The sales budget is constructed by multiplying the budgeted sales in units by the selling price. The information in the sales budget comes from a variety of sources.

Most of the detail for existing products comes from those personnel who deal with them on a day-to-day basis. The marketing manager contributes sales promotion information, which can alter the timing and amount of sales. The engineering and marketing managers may also contribute information about the introduction date of new products, as well as the retirement date of old products. The chief executive officer may revise these figures for the sales of any subsidiaries or product lines that the company plans to terminate or sell during the budget period.

**Example or Sample of a Sales Budget:**

Following is the sales budget of Hampton Freeze Inc. (see explanation of this budget)

HAMPTON FREEZE, INC.
Sales Budget
For the Year Ended December 31, 2003

| | Quarter | | | | |
|---|---|---|---|---|---|
| | 1 | 2 | 3 | 4 | Year |
| Budgeted sales in cases | 10,000 | 30,000 | 40,000 | 20,000 | 100,000 |
| Selling price per case | $ 20.00 | $ 20.00 | $ 20.00 | $ 20.00 | $ 20.00 |
| Total sales | $ 200,000 | $600,000 | $800,00 | $400,000 | 2,000,000 |
| | — | — | — | — | — |
| Percentage of sales collected in the period of the sales | | | 70% | | |
| Percentage of sales collected in the period after the sales | | | 30% | | |
| | 70% | 30% | | | |

**Schedule of Expected Cash Collections**

| | | | | | |
|---|---|---|---|---|---|
| 1 Accounts receivable, beginning balance | $90,000 | | | | $90,000 |
| 2 First quarter sales | 140,000 | $60,000 | | | 200,000 |
| 3 Second quarter sales | | 420,000 | $180,000 | | 600,000 |
| 4 Third quarter sales | | | 560,000 | $240,000 | 800,000 |
| 5 Fourth quarter sales | | | | 280,000 | 280,000 |
| 6 Total cash collections | $230,000 | $480,000 | $740,000 | $520,000 | $1,970,000 |
| | — | — | — | — | — |

1 Cash collections from last years fourth-quarter sales.

2 $200,000 × 70%; $200,000 × 30%

3 $600,000 × 70%; $600,000 × 30%

4 $800,000 × 70%; $800,000 × 30%

5 $400,000 × 70%

6 Uncollected fourth quarter sales appear as accounts receivable on the company's end of year balance sheet.

## Explanation of sales budget for Hampton Freeze Inc.

This example contains the sales budget for Hampton Freeze for the year 2009, by quarters. Notice from the example that the company plans to sell 100,000 cases of popsicles during the year, with sales peaking in the third quarter.

After preparing sales budget, a schedule of expected cash collections is also prepared such as the one that appear in our example. Cash collections consists of sales made to customers in prior periods plus collections on sales made in the current budget period. In our example, 70% of sales are collected in the quarter in which the sales are made and the remaining 30% are collected in the following quarter. For example, 70% of the first quarter sales of $200,000 (or

140,000) is collected during the first quarter and 30% (or $60,000) is collected during the second quarter.

**Example of the Sales Budget**

ABC Company plans to produce an array of plastic pails during the upcoming budget year, all of which fall into a single product category. Its sales forecast is outlined as follows:

ABC Company

Sales Budget

For the Year Ended December 31, 20XX

| | Quarter 1 | Quarter 2 | Quarter 3 | Quarter 4 |
|---|---|---|---|---|
| Forecasted unit sales | 5,500 | 6,000 | 7,000 | 8,000 |
| x Price per unit | $10 | $10 | $11 | $11 |
| Total gross sales | $55,000 | $60,000 | $77,000 | $88,000 |
| - Sales discounts & allowances | $1,100 | $1,200 | $1,540 | $1,760 |
| = Total net sales | $53,900 | $58,800 | $75,460 | $86,240 |

ABC's sales manager expects that increased demand in the second half of the year will allow it to increase its unit price from $10 to $11. Also, the sales manager expects that the company's historical sales discounts and allowances percentage of two percent of gross sales will continue through the budget period.

This example of the sales budget is simplistic, since it assumes that the company only sells in one product category. In reality, this example might have been a detail page that rolls up into the main sales budget, where it would occupy a single line item.

## *Other Sales Budget Issues*

It is not customary to include a calculation of cash receipts as part of the sales budget. Instead, the cash receipts are calculated for all of the revenues and expenditures of a business as a whole, and are then summarized on a separate page of the budget.

**Sales Management has the following key roles**

1) Hire, fire, and train sales staff - selection, maintenance and training of the sales staff is key to any company's success. Sales

managers must hire sales staff the can competently manage the sales process and meet or exceed quota. The Sales Manager must train and motivate the staff to perform. The Sales Manager must also replace underreporting sales staff. On going training is key to understanding the company sales process, sales value propositions and product sets.

2) Develop and manage sales territories and quotas, and manage any conflicts that arise as a result of customer, territory, quota or commission questions
3) Develop and implement sales compensation plans
4) Create, document and train in the company sales process
5) Interact with all departments that contribute to product delivery and support, customer service and finance.
6) Prepare and manage a sales budget in line with company financial objectives.
7) Coach sales staff to maximize their professional performance
8) Plan and facilitate regular sales meetings to keep staff and rest of company informed, energized and motivated.

## *Budget Process*

- In order to reach a consensus on annual spending limits and revenue sources, local, state, and national democratic governments must typically undergo a yearly series of hearings and negotiations to settle on a compromise budget. This is referred to collectively as a budget process. This can take days, weeks, or months, depending on a number of factors - most importantly, the fiscal status of a government.
- Generally, a budget process begins with a government's chief executive, be it a city's mayor, a state's governor, or a country's president submitting a draft budget. In local and state governments that run on a July 1 to June 30 fiscal year, this first budget proposal is normally offered in February or March. In one form or another, this budget is then introduced as a bill or resolution in the government's legislative branch.

- Appropriations hearings and initial negotiations then take place over the following months, with revenue figures for April and May - the months for which personal and business taxes are submitted - having particular influence in guiding the process. Following these hearings, public debate and private negotiations ensue between legislative leaders and the executive branch. Many states have constitutional requirements to pass a budget before the start of the fiscal year for which it applies, so there is often pressure for a budget to be passed by June 30. Once agreement is reached, the original budget bill is either amended to fit the final agreement, or a new version is introduced and quickly passed.
- At the federal level of the United States, which stands as the model for many countries, the fiscal year begins in October and ends in September. The budget process begins with a budget request being submitted by the president in February. This request includes funding requirements for each of the executive departments, as well as independent agencies, such as the Environmental Protection Agency (EPA). It also includes revenue proposals, such as new taxes and other ways to make money.
- Following this proposal, committees in both the U.S. House of Representatives and the Senate draft budget resolutions, which serve as either confirmations or counter-proposals to the president's request. Any discrepancies between the House and Senate versions are ironed out, in what is known as a conference committee, which consists of members from each chamber who negotiate compromise language.
- Importantly, at the federal level, the budget resolution is not law. Rather, it is a concurrent resolution that merely guides Congress. Individual appropriations bills for each of the spending areas must be passed, and be signed by the president for any spending to be legally authorized. There are roughly a dozen appropriations bills that account for the entirety of the federal government.

- No two budget processes are alike. Governments deep in debt, or with no strong legislative majority in place, may find themselves in a protracted budget process, while wealthy governments, or those with strong majorities, may reach spending and revenue agreements quickly. Current events may lend themselves to more or less popular support for various spending initiatives, new taxes, or cuts. In addition, governments with a strong party majority will be able to build a consensus quickly. In bicameral governments, having both chambers being led by the same party means a budget can be pushed through along party line votes, despite any opposition.

### *Importance of Sales Budget*

Sales budgets come in macro and micro versions, with the former projecting sales figures and expenses and the latter allocating marketing dollars to sales efforts. However you've chosen to organize your company -- you might have a marketing department that manages your sales function or independent sales and marketing functions -- creating sales budgets helps you in a variety of ways, including managing cash flow better and taking advantage of sales rep expertise.

Determining Overhead : Creating a specific budget for sales helps you determine your overhead costs, letting you see potential profit margins to set pricing strategies. Some businesses include all non-manufacturing costs in one overhead category, while others divide overhead between general and administrative and sales costs. If you use a sales budget as a projection of revenue and expenses, this helps you plan many or all of your other budget areas, especially if you create each budget based on revenue projections.

Better Cash Flow Management: When sales are good, some businesses increase their marketing spending, either using a formula that ties increases in spending to increases in sales or using a case-by-case decision-making process. When sales drop, it might be necessary to reduce your sales budget to stay profitable. This can lead to a further decrease in sales. Breaking out your sales expense can help you make targeted cuts in overhead that don't make marketing cuts that decrease sales. If your sales budget includes sales projections, this helps you plan for materials, labor, warehousing, shipping and production needs.

Maximizes Expertise: If you give your sales reps discretionary budgets, each rep can spend his budget based on aspects of his clients, territory and knowledge of the marketplace. For example, one rep might increase sales with trips to trade shows, while another might use a client newsletter or annual thank-you gifts to retain customers and increase their spending.

## *Types of Budget*

In order to properly plan and set goals, several different budgets must be created. This article discusses some of the more common budgets used by businesses.

Sales Budget - The sales budget is an estimate of future sales, often broken down into both units and dollars. It is used to create company sales goals.

Production Budget - Product oriented companies create a production budget. It is an estimate of the number of units that must be manufactured in order to meet the sales goals. The production budget also estimates the various costs involved with manufacturing those units, such as labor, material, and other expenses.

Cash Flow Budget - The cash flow budget is a prediction of future cash receipts and expenditures for a particular time period. It usually covers a period in the short term future. The cash flow budget helps the business determine when income will be sufficient to cover expenses and when the company will need to seek outside financing.

Marketing Budget - The marketing budget is an estimate of the funds needed for promotion, advertising, and public relations in order to market the product or service.

Project Budget - The project budget is a prediction of the costs associated with a particular company project. These costs include labor, materials, and other related expenses. The project budget is often broken down into specific tasks, with task budgets assigned to each.

Capital Budget - The capital budget is a prediction of company needs in regard to fixed assets, such as buildings, vehicles, machinery, and other equipment. It includes the cost of upgrading present assets, the cost of acquiring new assets, costs associated with maintenance of the assets, and fees associated with the assets. The capital budget helps the company plan for the acquisition and upkeep of these assets, which may include use of available cash or outside financing.

Master Budget - The master budget is a summary of the plans created for the subunits of the company. It is used to create projected financial statements. The master budget results in the creation of a pro forma income statement and a pro forma balance sheet. These are also referred to as a budgeted income statement and a budgeted balance sheet. Potential investors and lenders want to see the projected financial statements in order to make decisions that will ultimately affect the company.

## *Selling and Administrative Expense Budget*

### Definition and Explanation

Selling and administrative expense budget lists the budgeted expenses for areas other than manufacturing. In large organizations this budget would be a compilation of many smaller, individual budgets submitted by department heads and other persons responsible for selling and administrative expenses. For example, the marketing manager in a large organization would submit a budget detailing the advertising expenses for each budget period.

### Example

Following is the selling and administrative expense budget for Hampton Freeze Inc. (See explanation of this budget)

Hampton Freeze Inc.

Selling and Administrative Expense Budget

For the Year Ended December 31, 2009

| | Quarter 1 | 2 | 3 | 4 | Year |
|---|---|---|---|---|---|
| Budgeted sales in cases (see sales budget) | 10,000 | 30,000 | 40,000 | 20,000 | 100,000 |
| Variable selling and administrative expenses per case | $1.80 | $1.80 | $1.80 | 1.80 | $1.80 |
| Budgeted variable expense | $ 18,000 | $54,000 | $72,000 | $36,000 | $180,000 |
| Budgeted fixed selling and administrative expenses: | | | | | |
| Advertising | 20,000 | 20,000 | 20,000 | 20,000 | 80,000 |
| Executive salaries | 55,000 | 55,000 | 55,000 | 55,000 | 220,000 |
| Insurance | | 1,900 | 37,750 | | 39,650 |
| Property taxes | | | | 18,150 | 18,150 |
| Depreciation | 10,000 | 10,000 | 10,000 | 10,000 | 40,000 |
| Total budgeted fixed selling and administrative exp. | 85,000 | 86,900 | 122,750 | 103,150 | 397,800 |
| Total budgeted selling and administrative expenses | 103,000 | 140,900 | 194,750 | 139,150 | 577,800 |
| Less depreciation | 10,000 | 10,000 | 10,000 | 10,000 | 40,000 |
| Cash disbursements for selling and administrative exp. | $93,000 | $130,900 | $184,750 | $129,150 | $537,800 |

**Explanation of 'Selling and Administrative Expense Budget' for Hampton Freeze Inc.**

Like the manufacturing overhead budget the selling and administrative expense budget is divided into variable and fixed cost components. In the above example the variable selling and administrative expense is $1.80 per case. Consequently, budgeted sales in cases for each quarter are entered at the top of the schedule. These data are taken from the sales budget (see sales budget). The budgeted variable selling and administrative expenses are determined by multiplying the budgeted sales in cases by the variable selling and administrative expense per case. For example, the budgeted variable selling and administrative expense for the first quarter is $18,000 (10,000 cases × $1.80 per case). The fixed selling and administrative expenses (all given data) are then added to the variable selling and administrative expenses to arrive at the total budgeted selling and administrative expenses. Finally, to determine the cash disbursement for selling and administrative items, total budgeted selling and administrative expense is adjusted by adding back non-cash selling and administrative expenses (in this case, just depreciation).

## PROCEDURE OF SALES BUDGET

### *List of Products or Services*

- A sales budget will have a detailed layout and list of each of the products or services offered in the business. This type of budget will show how much each product or service offered through the company's product and service line is earning the business on a monthly basis. For example, the budget may have a single line per product and service, so the reader can easily find out how much the product is selling for, how much it costs to produce and how many quantities are being sold on a monthly basis. This type of sales budget should be updated and printed monthly, so executives can use the information for financial planning.

### *Production Fees*

- As mentioned in the previous section, the sales budget must show detailed information regarding the product or service. This includes the production fees. A product may cost a specific amount to produce, because it uses specific tools or supplies that may need to be imported. The production fees may also include labor cost, but whether or not it is included in the sales budget is up to the budget creators and executives. Services, such as website development and design, may not cost much in production but can be costly in terms of software programs or membership fees that need to be paid for the business to use specific design programs, for example.

*Testing*

- Depending on the product or service being created by the business, it may be subject to testing before it hits the market for sale. For example, any baby toys or products that could be potentially dangerous to users must be tested to ensure it is safe to use for those who the product is designed for. Services must also be tested, as a website needs to be fully functional before it is launched and given to the user. Depending on the testing in question, it may require some additional fees, which needs to be included in the sales budget.

*Maintenance and Updates*

- Once the sales budget has been completed with the relevant information, an accountant or sales manager must update the budget on a monthly basis to ensure that all figures and sales totals are truthful and accurate. The information is not only used by the sales manager to determine whether the budget is maintained, but also used by executives to plan ahead and make changes to the existing products or product line.

## BUDGET PURPOSES

The budget is an important factor in the successful operation of the sales force. Top sales managers spend a great deal of time attempting to convince corporate management to increase the size of their budget. Budgets are formulated for many reasons, including the major ones of planning, co-ordination & control.

Planning: Corporations and their functional units develop objectives for future periods and budgets determine how these objectives will be met. For example alternative marketing plans, the probable profit from each plan and individual budget for each will be considered before management is able to decide on future management programs.

Co-ordination: The budget is the major management tool for coordinating the activities of all functional areas and sub-groups within the entire organization. For example sales must be co-ordinated with production to ensure that enough products are available to meet demand. The production manager can use sales forecast and the sales department's marketing plans to determine the necessary production level. Budgeting allows the financial executive to determine the firm's revenues & expenses and have enough capital to finance all business operations.

Control Allocation of budgeted funds gives management control over their use. Sales managers estimate their budget needs, are given funds to operate their units and then are held responsible for reaching their stated goals by using their budgets effectively. As the sales program is implemented and income and expenses are actually generated, managers assess results against the amount budgeted and determine whether they are meeting objectives.

Methods: How much money does the sales manager receive to operate the sales force?

Although no fixed financial formulas exist to appropriate funds, firms use one of the three general methods to determine how money should be allocated.

First, some firms use an arbitrary percentage of sales.

Second, other firms may use executive judgement.

Third, a few companies estimate the cost of operating each sales force unit along with the cost of each sales program over a specific period to arrive at a total budget. Which ever method is chosen the actual amount budgeted will be based on the organization's sales forecast, marketing plans, projected profits, top management's perception of the sales force's importance in reaching corporate objectives, and the sales manager's skill in negotiating with superiors.

Budgets are often modified several times before the final dollar figures are estimated.

**These Questions should be answered**

- How much can you realistically sell next year?
- How much will you charge for your goods or services?
- How much will it cost to produce your product?
- How much are your operating expenses?
- Do you need to hire employees? If so, how many, and how much will you pay them?
- How much will you pay yourself?
- How much payroll tax and unemployment tax will you pay?
- How much money do you need to borrow, and how much will your monthly loan payments be?
- The answers to these questions will form the basis of your budget and forecast.

## *Choosing a Budget Method*

A budget is nothing more than a written estimate of how an organization - or a particular project, department, or business unit - will perform financially. If you can accurately predict your company's performance, you can be certain that resources such as money, people, equipment, manufacturing plants, and the like are deployed appropriately.

## *Kinds of budgets*

When it comes right down to it, you can budget any activity in your organization that has a financial impact. Two of the most common budgets are

- Cash budget: An estimate of a company's cash position for a particular period of time.
- Operating budget: A business's forecasted revenues along with forecasted expenses, usually for a period of one year or less.

Line items in your operating budget may include:

- Labor budget: The total labor cost to be expended for a set period of time calculated by taking every person in an organization, department, or project and multiplying the number of hours they are expected to work by their wage rates.
- Sales budget: An estimate of the quantity of goods and services that will be sold during a specific period of time.
- Production budget: A forecast thatstarts with the sales budget's estimates of the total number of units projected to be sold, then translates this information into estimates of the cost of labor, material, and other expenses required to produce them.
- Expense budget: An estimate prepared for travel, utilities, office supplies, telephone, and many other common business expenses for a given period.
- Capital budget: The total costs and maintenance fees planned for your company's fixed assets.

The best kind of budget is the one that works. You can choose from three key approaches to developing a budget:

- Top down: Budgets are prepared by top management and imposed on the lower layers of the organization. Top down budgets clearly express the performance goals and expectations of top management, but can be unrealistic because they do not incorporate the input of the very people who implement them.
- Bottom up: Supervisors and middle managers prepare the budgets and then forward them up the chain of command for review and approval. These budgets tend to be more accurate and can have a positive impact on employee morale because employees assume an active role in providing financial input to the budgeting process.
- Zero-based budgeting: Each manager prepares estimates of his or her proposed expenses for a specific period of time as though they were being performed for the first time. In other words, each activity starts from a budget base of zero. By starting from scratch at each budget cycle, managers are required to take a close look at all their expenses and justify them to top management, thereby minimizing waste.

Budget tricks of the trade

When your expenditures exceed your budget, you can do several things to get back on track:

- Review your budget. Before you do anything else, take a close look at your budget and make sure that the assumptions on which it is based are accurate and make sense in your changing market. If your market is growing quickly, you may need to adjust up your estimates. Sometimes, it's the budget - not the spending - that is out of line.
- Freeze spending. One of the quickest and most effective ways to bring spending back in line with a budget is to freeze expenses such as pay raises, new staff, and bonuses.
- Postpone new projects. New projects, including new product development, acquisition of new facilities, and research and development, can eat up a lot of money. However, if you are too zealous in curbing spending when you need to develop new products or services to compete, the result can be disastrous for the future growth and prosperity of the company.
- Lay off employees and close facilities. This is the last resort when you're trying to cut expenses. Although these actions will result in an immediate and lasting decrease in expenses, you also face an immediate and lasting decrease in the talent available to your organization. Productivity and morale of remaining employees may also suffer.

### *Funding of Sales Budget*

It implies the inputs in financial terms required to achieve a particular level of sales. Level of sales budget implies level of spending on different activities like personal selling, advertising, sales-promotions and public relations including publicity. Besides promotion mix , communication mix also plays vital role in determining sales budget like personal selling or through net, telephone, wholesalers and retailers or other medium. The inputs of funding involves two types of costs:

1) fixed cost - It includes salary and other administration expanses like sales building , furniture and fixture put there in.
2) Variable cost- It includes expenses like incentives to sales staff, commission/ discount to buyers, travelling expense, boarding and lodging expense, advertising and publicity expense etc

### *Funding of Sales Force*

It is made by Finance Department after verifying the projections of sales and corresponding expenditure to be incurred to achieve the same. It is pertinent to mention that most of expenses are incurred before hand the achievement of sales .It also depends on sales of past few months. It basically deals with personal selling activities and sales force

### *Methods of Funding Sales Force*

Percentage of Sales Method - This method is quiet simple and is determined by multiplying sales revenue by given percentage determined in advance of taking into account importance of promotion mix.

**Merit**

1) VERY simple, easy to understand and interpret
2) Time saving

**Demerit**

1) Result is based on percentage and not on any rational thinking
2) This method does not satisfy cause and effect relationship

Competitive Method Parity- This method takes into consideration the practices of the competitors in regard to their selling and promotional activities. Competitive practices serve as their guide in setting sales spending levels. Such practice might refer to either a particular competitor or to any industry average.

**Merit**

1) It is very simple method

2) It gives tough competiton to its rival if budget is correctly prepared

**Demerit**

1) Seriously effected by Economies of firm
2) This technique may neglect company objectives
3) A company which is financially not too big than its rivals may collapse

Affordable Method - In this method ,management will first decide the revenue over total cost of goods sold. The next decision would be to determine what share of this excess, the company is prepared to spend on selling and administration cost , after achieving predetermined level of profit

**Merit**

1) It is based on logical and rational approach
2) It provides very simple and self explanatory solution

**Demerit**

1) It neglects differential yields of selling expenditure

Objective and Task Method- This approach starts with sales objectives to be attained during plan period and involves 4 steps

Step One- It is used to identify objectives to be achieved by selling force during planned period

Step Two- It involves various tasks or activities which are necessary to be carried out to realize inputs required to reach objectives

Step Three- It is used to translate the activities into expenditure estimating amount required to be spent on each activity

Step Four- It involves adding up all selling costs warranted by objectives according to territory

**Merit**

1) Gives weight age to Sales Objective
2) It sounds most appropriate method

**Demerit**

1) Very difficult to compute precisely to execute certain tasks

## BIBLIOGRAPHY

http://www.accounting4management.com/sales_budget.htm

https://www.google.co.in/search?q=sales+ budget&tbm=isch&tbo=u&source=univ&sa=X&ei=l-eOUqPy DYPqrQfry YEo&sqi=2&ved=0CCoQsAQ

http://www.accountingtools.com/sales-budget

http://books.google.co.in/books?id=xk4s UNWQPxcC&pg=PA325&lpg=PA325&dq=nature+of+sales+ budget&source=bl&ots=m AamB63x9J&sig=x-2D

http://www.wisegeek.com/what-is-the-budget-process.htm

http://voices.yahoo.com/what-types-budgets-businesses-use-317468.html?cat=3

http://www.slideshare.net/indranshgupta/sales-budget-quotas-and-sales-territories

http://smallbusiness.chron.com/sales-budget-important-60445.html

http://www.accounting4management.com/selling_and_admn_expenses_budget.htm

http://www.scribd.com/doc/28091461/Sales-Budget

http://www.dummies.com/how-to/content/choosing-a-budget-method.html

# SALES ORGANIZATION

## INTRODUCTION AND MEANING:

Whenever two or more persons join together to do activities for achieving some common objectives, a necessity to distribute the work among them is felt and coordination among different activities is to be made. The organization originates from this very necessity. Organization is the process of identifying and grouping the work to be performed, defining and delegating responsibility and establishing relationship for the purpose of enabling people to work together most efficiently in attaining objectives.

Sales organization is a structured framework, specifying the formal authority and responsibility among persons working in the organization. It consists of group of individuals working to achieve selling objectives to increase sales, maximizing profits, expanding market share etc. it establishes coordination among various selling activities necessary for the achievement of selling objectives.

Sales organization is not a separate unit. It is affected by other functional areas such as production, finance, personnel etc. Sales organization organizes group of persons in the form of a suitable structure, depending upon the requirements of the enterprise. Various forms of sales organization structure can be line organization, line and staff organization functional sales organization, committee form of sales organization.

### *Definition:*

According to H.R. Toosdal, "A sales organization consists of human beings working together for the marketing of products manufactured by the firm or marketing of commodities which have been purchased for resale."

According to Still and Cundiff, "A sales organization is group of individual striving jointly to reach certain goals and bearing formal as well as informal relations to each other."

According to American Marketing Association, "Sales organization is the planning, directing and coordinating the activities of sales force for increasing organizational efficiency."

### *Characteristics of Sales Organization:*

Sales organization has the following characteristics:

1. Sales organization is a part of the total enterprise.
2. It works for the attainment of common selling objectives like maximizing sales volume, maximizing profits, increasing market shares etc.
3. It consists of group of people engagement in selling activities like distribution, sales-promotion, personal-selling, advertising, etc.
4. It defined the duties, responsibilities and rights of people engaged in selling activities and coordinate their activities.
5. It establishes formal and informal relationships among persons engaged in selling activities.
6. The success of sales organization depends on the unified and coordinated efforts of sales personnel.
7. The sales organization works under the direct control of General Sales Manager.

**Sales Organization Flow Chart**

Factors Affecting the Size / Structure of Sales Organization

1. Nature of the product: nature of the product plays an important role in determining the structure of sales organization.
2. Area of Operation / Market Area: if the product is sold locally, sales organization will be small. And if the market is large the organization will be large

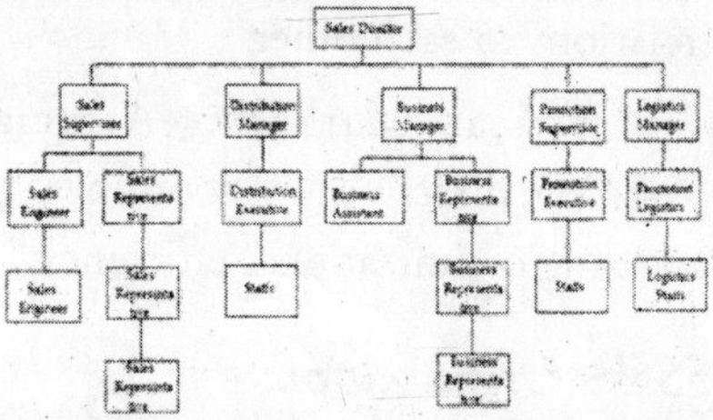


3. Size of the Enterprise: Large enterprises have large sales organization e.g. Reliance telecom has large sales org.
4. Number of products: If the enterprise is dealing with large number of products, it needs large sales organization. E.g. Hindustan levers is selling many products like Lipton tea , lux soap , lifebuoy soap, while company which is selling few products will have small sales organization
5. Distribution policy:Different companies follow different different distribution policies for their products directly to the customers opening their own shop or through their personal selling.
6. Level of competition: if the level competition is high in the market , many salesman have appointed to attract the customers so the size of the sales organization becomes large
7. Tradition and customs: Tradition and customs prevailing in similar types of business units also affects the structure of sales organization. When the new business is set up, then while deciding structure of the organization we should consider the prevailing traditions and form of sales organizational structure of sales organization. When a new business is set up, then while

deciding structure of sales organization structure of existing business unit in the same industry in the same geographical locations.

8. Sales policies: if the business unit adopts the aggressive sales policy then it will require more salesmenfor achieving higher sales level. The business units who sell goods on credit, installment system, hire purchases system will have to employee more salesmen for collecting dues, installments from customers.
9. Ability ofTop-officials: If top-officials of the institute are highly educated, experienced, skilled, efficient, and then business unit can adopt line sales organization, because these experienced officers can take necessary decisions without the help of experts.

### *Principles of sales organization:*

1. Principle of Unity of Objectives: Success of sales organization is measured by the success of its objectives. So the objectives of the sales organization should be clearly defined so that every part of sales organization tries to achieve them. The principle of unity of objective means that even if the various units of sales organization have different aims, they are somehow or the other linked with the main objective of sales organization.
2. Principle of Specialization: According to this principle, the sales organization should be established in such a manner that work is divided among individuals according to their knowledge, experience, taste. Such a division of work makes every person a specialist in his field.
3. Principle of coordination: All the departments established under sales organization are inter-dependent. If there is some hindrance in the functioning of one department, the sales organization may be affected.
4. Principle of Parity of Authority and Responsibility: According to this principle, whatever responsibility is given to an individual, he should be given an equal amount of authority to discharge his responsibility.

5. Principle of exception: According to this, superior should retain the authority to take decisions regarding important activities alone, and the authority to take decisions on routine matter should be delegated to subordinates.

## *Significance of Sales Organization:*

a). **To plan purchase:**

The firm's sales are depending on the sales prospects of it. Consumer is the boss who decides the dimension of what he want, where he want, at what cist he want and so on. This boss in the king pin and in thefirm will have to understand product planning and development accordingly.

b). **To create a pattern of demands for products:**

The products of the firm are not sold themselves. Somebody must be there to push them form the shelves to the Bags of the customers; such push is not physical one; it is psychological. Salesman does it directly and advertising indirectly.

c). **To handle the orders received:**

Selling routine calls for highly specialized tasks of receiving enquiries, entertaining them with latest and least quotations, appearing for orders, receiving orders, packing the products as per the instruction of the customers, dispatching them to the expectation s of the buyers-may be individuals or organizations. All these are crucial and constructive tasks.

d). **To collect the dues:**

Credit sales from the bulk share in these days of fast moving competition. If one only speaks of hard cash business, the sales organization has to pull the shutters down because, credit is the breath of economic transactions. Collection of dues is like performing a tight rope dance where utmost care is to be taken to maintain the balance which is the secret of success.

e). **To handle the task of personal management:**

Management of sales force demands good many activities. Sales-force is to be selected, trained, placed, transferred, promoted, motivated, maintained and controlled. These aspects require investment in terms of talent, time, and treasure.

## *Types of Sales Organization*

Organization is an entity designed to identify and group the work to be performed, defining and delegating the authorities and responsibilities and establishing relationships to enable the people within the organization to work with efficiency and effectiveness towards the attainment of the general and specific goals. There are four very prominent types. These are functional, product, consumer and area type.

1. **Functional Type:**

   In case of functional type of organization it is classified and divided and sub divided on the basis of functions to be performed. It take the following shape as shown:

**EVALUATION:**

**MERITS:**

(1) Specialization at different levels.

(2) Flexibility of increasing and decreasing of departments as per needs.

(3) Quick decision making.

(4) Easy co-ordination between sub functions.

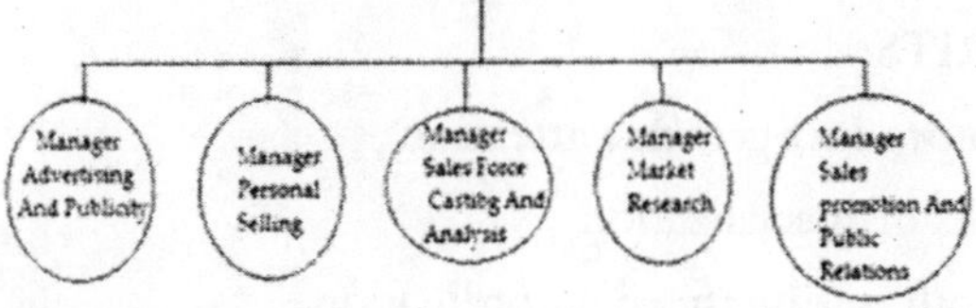


(5) Economical

**DEMERITS:**

(1) Products do not get due attention.

(2) Delay because of sub division of departments.

(3) Problem of co-ordination due to increased responsibility of general manager.

(4) Conflicts between departments.

(5) Effectiveness of organization is badly affected due to malfunctioning of departments.

**SUITABILITY:** Functional Departmentalization is suitable when:

(1) Size of the organization is small.

(2) Where limited number of products are there.

(3) Where there is minor difference in technology of productions.

2. **Product Type:**

In case of product type, the departmentation is based on the types of the products where for each product functional division can be possible. It looks like:

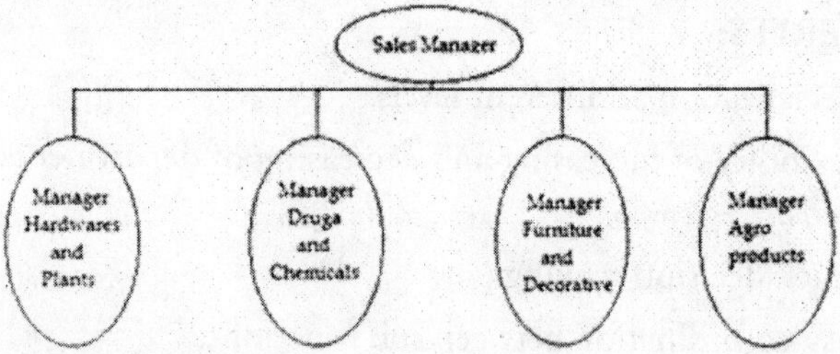


EVALUATION:

MERITS:

(1) Each product gets due attention.

(2) Merits of specialization.

(3) Smooth un-interfered co-ordination.

(4) Easy assignment of responsibility.

(5) Possibility of comparative efficiency.

DEMERITS:

(1) Problem of co-ordination between product department.

(2) Increased selling cost.

(3) High cost of operations.

(4) Self-contained unit.

(5) No brake on freedom of employees.

**SUITABILITY:** Product departmental organization is suitable where

(1) Too many products are there.

(2) Where products are highly priced.

(3) Where products are of technical nature.

**3. Consumer Specialization Type:**

In case of consumer specialization, the basis of departmentation will be the types of consumers to be served. Many a times, market features are more important. Then the organization takes the following shape

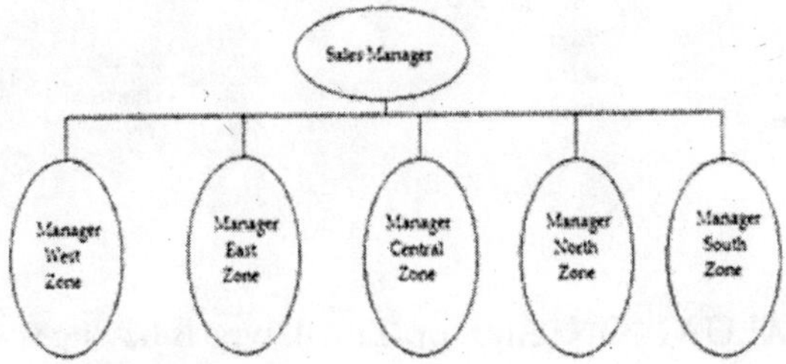


EVALUATION:

MERITS:

(1) Each category of consumer gets due attention.

(2) Maximum service to the consumers.

(3) Better sales planning and policies keeping each category at focus.

(4) Specialized salesmen to meet the requirements ofcostumers.

(5) Company image building.

DEMERITS:

(1) Higher establishment expenses.

(2) Problems of co-ordination control of sales activities.

(3) Duplication of efforts and investments.

**SUITABILITY:** Consumer specialization type of organization is suitable where

(1) Too many customers are there requiring a special treatment.

(2) When company has all types of customer work caring for.

**4. Area Type:**

Geographic or area wise departs mentation is recorded to meet the changing consumption attributes of areas. Such an organization looks like:

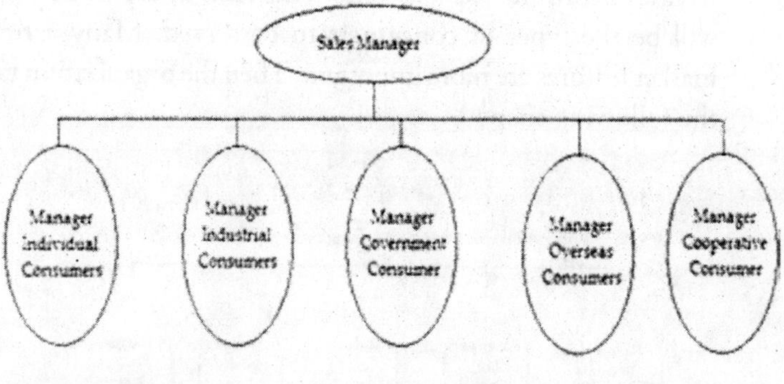


**EVALUATION:** Area' or 'Zonal' type is having the merits:

**MERITS:**

(1) Better service to customers,

(2) New and modified products can be provided.

(3) Transport cost can be reduced.

(4) Zonal competition can be combated.

(5) Zonal sales performance can be measured for betterment.

**DEMERITS:**

(1) It is a costly proposition.

(2) Problem of co-ordination of different markets.

(3) Greater conflicts for resource allocation and facilities.

**SUITABILITY:** Zonal structure is suitable where:

(1) Market territory is large and substantive.

(2) Each market is different.

(3) Products can be differentiated on quality zonal wise.

(4) Total sales much higher.

## FUNCTIONS OF A SALES MANAGER

The basic aim of sales manager is to promote sales and contribute to the profits of the concern on one hand and satisfaction to consumer on other hand. In big concerns, sales manager is generally assisted by different personnel in the sales line. In smaller concern, he is all alone with a skeleton service of subordinate. Notwithstanding these differences, a sales manager is to perform following functions:

1. **Planning the future sales:**

   Sales' planning is one of the most dominant functions of sales management which seeks to achieve co-ordinated structure of operations of various programs in relation to sales.

   To plan is to look ahead. It is the process of thinking before doing. He is to plan for long range. A sale budgeting is the instrument of sales planning that gives items like product wise, sales for the year and years to come.

2. **Selection and placement of salesmen:**

   Any successful sales organization warrants the selection of men capable of accelerating the wheels of it. "Right men for the right points" is the watch word for a dynamic sales manager. Scientific selection is a rigorous process or a hurdle race designed by a sales manager which is to be won by the salesman. Selection procedure embraces minute and meticulous stages such as - calling for interview - testing them - conduct of medical examination-and the final interview and appointment.

3. **Direction and co-ordination of sales-force:**

   Management is essentially an art of getting the work done. The Sales manager is responsible not only for planning organizing the sales activities, but also for guiding and supervising his sales subordinates. He is the leader who is to direct his sub-ordinates by issuing necessary orders, guiding and reading and supervising their activities as the part of performance. Naturally superiority complex plays its icy hands; misunderstanding creep in. therefore, there is need for bringing about unity of thought, purpose and action in the ranks and files. Coordination is opposite of conflict. Coordination kills conflict by timing, balancing and integrating the variables.

4. **Organizing the sales organization:**

   Having planned the various activities, the sales manager is to decide as to how and who will perform these activities. Organization is the process of the framework of relations in the unit that is geared to attain the objective of undertaking. It involves a critical and in-depth study of actual requirements of organization, division of it into viable departments, designing the lines of authority and responsibility and the delegation of authorities to sub-ordinates to get going.

5. **Advertising the Top Management:**

   Mere planning of sales activities is not the responsibilities of a sales manager. He is accountable for the actual happenings in his department which are to be reported to the top management. He is to advise on opening and closing of branches. He is also to advise the higher officials of opportunities and threats of venture; new appointment and, selection, transfers, promotions; on pricing and discount policies and show their bearings on profitability and profits of the unit.

6. **Training the Sales-Force:**

   Motivation and morale are the primary purposes of training. Training improves employee productivity, standardizes working procedure for the sales-force, reduces personnel turn over, provides rescue force of trained and experienced men and women and instills the confidence of performance par excellence. Sales manager is to plan for training new employee and continuing it in case of experienced hands through refresher courses. A good plan of training embraces managerial supervision and service personnel in the sales organizations.

7. **Compensating the sales-force:**

   Sound employer and employee relations are the base for the total success of sales organization. There will be sweet relations between men and boss when the employer treats employees' well, pays well so that the employee put their heart and soul together to better the performance. The employee efforts are to be rewarded amply. Employee motivation and morale depend on compensation policy in consultation with personnel experts that is viable and workable. A good plan is one that pays well in time treats impartially, economical, productive and elastic.

8. **Controlling the sales force:**

   When the sales-force is provided with quality products, equipments, adequately compensated one can expert the best results. There is always gap between promises and performance due to the factor which are both controllable and uncontrollable. If everything goes well, there is no need for control. Control means having continuous watch on the working of any program and applying brakes or speed to actions wherever necessary.

## TYPES OF SALES MANAGERS

The sales manager can be classified in to certain categories mainly on the basis of the nature of the functions performed by them. Experts of modern management process have divided management in to two classes as "administrative" and "operative" management. Administrative management is basically a 'thinking' process and operative management is more concerned with 'doing'.

1. Administrative sales manager.
2. Operative Sales manager.
3. Administrative-cum-operative sales manager.

## DEPARTMENTS IN SALES ORGANIZATION

Sales organization may have following departments:

(1) Physical Distribution Department: This department performs the functions of storage, packing, dispatching and

transportation. This department has various sections like storage section, packing section, transportation section etc. Each section is headed by person having specialization in his field.

(2) Advertising Department: The function of this department is to plan advertising compaign, to select media of advertising keeping in mind nature of product, nature of customers, availability of funds, media cost, media circulation; and to implement advertising-programmes etc. It helps to increase sales by informing, persuading and reminding people about the goods and services.

(3) Personnel Department: A wing of personnel department works in the sales organization. This department performs the function of recruiting and selecting salesman, training them, placing them, motivating them, coordinating and controlling their activities etc. This is headed by personnelmanager. This department solves the problem related to human element in the sales organization.

(4) Public Relation Department: This department perfoms the function of knowing public opinion about the firm. It works to build positive image of the brand, product and firm. This department establishes contacts with customers, suppliers, employees, media, bankers, government officials, political leaders, social organizations, other competing and non-competing organizations. This department is headed by public relation officer. For success of business in the long run, good public relations are must and this department works to create and maintain good public relations.

(5) Sales Department: Sales department is a very important part of sales organization. The sales manager acts as the head of the sales department. In a big organization, he is considered as next to the top authority in the chain of command. In small organization there is no separate physical-distribution department and the debt collection department.

(6) Market Research Department: The main task of this department is to conduct research about consumer behavior. To measure

level of consumer satisfaction or dissatisfaction, to explore new markets, to collect information about exiting demand and supply, to measure effectiveness of advertisement, to find effective channels of distribution etc.

(7) Debt Collection Department: Now-a-days goods are sold on both cash and credit basis. The system of selling durable and semi-durable goods on installments is very common. These installments must be collected well in time to avoid risk of bad debts and loss of interest due to blockage of funds. For this the firm must have efficient debt collection department. This department tries to reduce debt collection period without disrupting relations with customers.

(8) Statics and Record Department: This department has two sections:

(i) Statistics section

(ii) Record section.

Statistics section collects data and information from present consumers, potential-consumers, market intermediaries, salesman etc. It collects information about sale, repeat sales, quantity demanded by customers, sales of competitive firms, percentage change in market share, etc.

Record department maintains and preserves this data in such a way that it can be readily available to the decision-makers. The data is stored in the form of papers, files, floppies, and other electronic devices. This data is useful for decision making and sales forecasting.

(3) Sales Promotion Department: Sales promotion is defined as those promotional activities that provide various incentives to the sales force, distributors, consumers for promoting sales. This department is headed by sales promotion manager. This department arranges various sales-promotion activities to promote sales.

## CONCLUSION:

The framework emphasizes close involvement of the sales organization in developing business and marketing strategy, rather than fulfilling the operational and implementation role of the past. The strategic sales organization will require a different infrastructure to that of the past, and many companies are struggling with the fact that conventional sales organizations were set up and designed to do a quite different job to that which is now required. It is found that the sales department has more influence than the marketing department on many so-called "marketing" decisions and that primary marketing coordinators increasingly reside in ales rather than the marketing organization, while sales plays a growing role in formulating as well as executing marketing strategies.

## REFERENCES:

1). Advertising And Sales Management, Dr. C.N.Sontakki

2). Advertising and Sales Management, Mukesh Trehan & Raju Trehan

3). Relationship Marketing: Theory & Practice, Francis Buttle

4). Google search

# RECRUITMENT AND SELECTION OF SALES FORCE ?

## INTRODUCTION

Recruitment and selection is an essential element of the activity center management underlying human resources: namely, the acquisition , development and rewarding workers. It is often an important part of the work of human resource managers - or designated specialists in work organizations. However, and importantly, recruitment and selection decisions are often made for good reason by non -specialists, by managers lines. It is therefore, an important sense in which it is the responsibility of all managers and where human resources services exist, it is possible that human resource managers play a more consultative role in supporting those who supervise or other ways to work with the new employee.

As Mullins (2010 , p 485) notes: " If the function of human resource management is to remain effective , there must always have a good level of teamwork and cooperation and consultation between line managers and the Director of Human resources courses . "This is certainly the case in the recruitment and selection of specialist HR managers (or even external consultants) may be an important reservoir of knowledge and skills up to date, on important legal dimensions of the region.

Recruitment and selection is often presented as a rational activity planned, including some phases sequentially linked in a process of staffing, which itself may be located within a strategy of human resource management in the broadest sense. Bratton and Gold differentiate the two terms while establishing a clear link between them as follows:

" Recruitment is the process of creating a pool of people able to apply for a job in an organization. The selection is the process by which managers and others use specific instruments to choose from a pool of candidates or those most likely to succeed in the job (s), taking into account management objectives and legal requirements. Establishing a similar distinction in which recruitment activities constitute a pool of people eligible for selection, Foot and Hook suggests that "although the two functions are closely related , each requires a separate set of skills and know-how , and in practice can be met by different staff members. Recruitment activity, but not normally the selection decision can be entrusted to an agency. It is therefore logical to treat each activity separately

## RECRUITMENT

**What is it?**

Recruitment is the process by which the candidate are traced and encouraged For the employee positions vacant in the organisation.

## STANDARD DEFINITIONS

Professor Edwin B. Flippo:

"Recruitment is the process of searching for prospective employee and stimulate them to apply for jobs in the organization

Professor Victor P. Bwell:

"Recruitment is the search for the best available candidate for a sales position".

Professor Dale Yoder:

"Recruitment is a process to discover the source of manpower to meet the requirement of the staffing schedule and to employ effective measures for attracting that manpower in adequate numbers to facilitate effective selection of an efficient working force".

Professors Byars and Rue:

"Recruitment involves seeking and attracting a pool of people from which qualified candidates for job vacancies can be chosen"

Recruitment is positive process encouraging the eligible candidates to apply for the posts to stand the chance of selection. It is one which concentrates on building and rebuilding are serve force of prospective employees.

### *Why recruitment?*

1. To fill the gaps created: Recruitment is necessary in all sales organisations in order To provide replacement for position vacated by resignations, disabilities, deaths, discharge, dismissals, retirement promotion and so on. If ready sales force is not available, it causes transitory loss to the firm both financial and non-financial.
2. To meet the recruitments of expansion: Birth, growth and expansion are the sure signs of progressive organisation. Firms are bound to grow as there are growth stimulants. A firm may start on a Small Scale, but being a adaptive one is sure to prosper and expand' diversify and further prosper ; it adds new product' lines ;it goes local to regional, regional to national and from national to international. Such growth and expansion programs warrant incoming or more and more sales personnel.

## IMPORTANCE OF RECRUITMENT

Sales mains rightly described as the "spearhead" of the company. It is a force direct hits. Creative professional sellers or sellers are the real assets of the sales organization that is ready for progress and prosperity. Pick and choose such talent, gifted sellers is a results of its recruitment policy. The goal is " Ought right man for postition WhLCl1 Orks rec This is the philosophy that recruitment on solving the problem of the labor principles of this philosophy are: thorough selection standards involving hi h qualifications and using all proven methods to choose vendors and `(selection i5g surface with the hope that some will succeed where sellers accept hired to work for the wages offered . If fundamental objective is set aside, the misfits replace crises incompetent sellers drift round to slow or engage in work without care where it is the absence of strict control. unfit These vendors, instead of building society and picture company , damage and drop nor his morale is high , or that allows others to enjoy high morale. Finally, the "show sales" must be closed sales decreased to low profits squeezed has round pegs in square holes are strange men and are in no way calling sellers value. Mistake in recruitment is a mistake and it is sure to cost a lot.

## ASPECTS OF RECRUITMENT

Recruitment as a positive process embraces three aspects namely, job analysis, personnel analysis and tapping the sources available. Let us see each aspects at length.

1 JOB ANALYSIS:

Job analysis is the maiden step in the procedure of recruitment. It is almost difficult, if for a sales manager to recruit and select a person in any position of sales organization unless he has the perfect knowledge of what type of job is to be given to a prospective employee in case he or she is selected. Here, it is job analysis that comes to his rescue. Job analysis is the study of what a salesman do?

2 PERSONNEL ANALYSIS:

If the job analysis is the description of job or gives job specifications, the personnel analysis speaks of employee specification or man specification. Job specification decided the qualifications and the qualities required for a post- maybe physical, mental, social and character The physical specification relate to age height, weight, appearance, voice, health specifications with educational qualification, intelligence, alertness, imagination, confidence initiative, observation; social qualities with extrovert, covering ability, poise courtesy, tactco operation, manners, character qualities with extrovert, covering ability , poise , courtesy, tact, industry determination and so on. Man analysis speaks of how much a candidate is possess these expected or standard quota of quality mix.

3. TAPPING RECRUITMENT SOURCES

After deciding the type and the number of employees needed based on job analysis, job specifications and job descriptions, the sales manager is to hunt the possible sources of recruitment The available sources of recruitment can be "internal" and "external".

## PROCESS OF RECRUITMENT OF SALES FORCE:

Recruitment is the continuous process and is the alpha function of the searching, placing, motivating and controlling the sales force. This recruitment being the first stage, hascertain definite steps. These are explained at length.

I. Determination of the Nature of Sales Force:

The nature of sales-people is determined on the basis of the job requirements. Salespeople are of different nature; some are creative and service oriented. Some prefer to sell goods to 'middle, still some directly to customers. Some prefer to work in local markets, some national markets and still some in international markets. That is why, the nature of salesmen is determined on the basis of job requirements. Here, two functions are basically involvedindetermining the nature and suitability of sales-people namely,

## JOB ANALYSIS AND REVIEW OF PRESENT SALES PEOPLE

**Job Analysis:** As noted as an aspect, of recruitment, job analysis is the process of studying the operations, duties and organisational aspects of jobs in order to derive specifications or as they are called by some, as job description. For analysing the job being carried out by salesmen following two significant activities are called for:

I. Job Description:

It is the process where to start with analysis of sales activities made and job description is prepared. Job description needs two kinds of information namely technique need and the working conditions. In so far as technical needs are concerned a thorough knowledge about the following are very essential: (a) Specification of the technical, knowledge about the products and services so that the sales-people may be able to undertake the sales effectively and (B) Specification of various technical information and facts so that sales people may be able to remove the objections of customers. Coming to working conditions, the information and facts so that sales people may be able to remove the objections of customers(a) the problems to be faced in selling (b) the expected volume of sales at present (c) estimate of future sales (d) the role, liability and mutual relation of salesperson

II. Man Specifications.

Man specification focusses light on employee needs such as (A) physical features - health, voice, attractive personality (b) mental qualities as level of education mental balance, curiosity, imagination and the like. (c) Social and moral qualities like obedience encouragement ,friendship, cooperation, sincerity and the like (d) capacity to bear the rights and responsibility , decision-making and so on (e) Actual work experience.

B Review of the Present Sales Personnel:

On the basis of mental and social qualities, the sales people are to be recruited

**Determination of the Number of Sales-people Required:**

After determining then nature of the sales-force, the next logical step is to determine the Number of sales people required to execute the sales job. Usually, the number of sales people

IS determined by keeping in view of the following facts: (1) Present sales activities of the firm (2) Future prospects for expansion of sales (3) Estimated sales by each salesman (4) Number of present salesmen to be promoted to higher posts (5) Expected number of sales people to leave the organisation either by retrenchment or by retirement on their own (6) The usual turnover rate of salesman(7) Nature and extent of competition. A formula is used to calculate the expected number of salesmen needed for future requirement.

N = S/P (1 + T)

Where

N = Number

S = Sales forecasts

P = Present average sales by salesman

T = Turnover of sales people.

This will be more clear if one takes an illustration. Say in the well known company ofM/s Everest Sales Private Limited following data is available from which calculate the number of sales people required. The company forecasts a sales of Rs. 10,00,00,000 for the next year.The present sales by an average sales person is of Rs. 2,50,000. The rate of turnover of salespeople is presently at 5 percent. The present strength of working sales people is 300 sales people.The need for additional sales people in the coming year will be :

N = 10,00,00,000/2,50,000 (1+5/200)

= 400 (1.05)

= 420 sales persons -rg

Net Number = 420 - 300 = 120 Sales people

0 Hence, the additional number of sales persons required are : 120 sales people for the

coming year.

**Determination of Sources of Sales Force :**

First of all, one approach is used lo evaluate the sources of recruits used in the post to the ratio of success and failures among the number of recruits produced One source may have provided numerous recruits, but u few successful, a sound, fewer recruits but high numbers of successful sales people.

1. Promotions:

As a matter of policy, firms employ sales from within by promoting the employee fromlower post to higher post. Vacancies other _than at lowest level are filled up by promotion the personnel at higher level. that is, a promotion leads to another promotion. It is a good step because, the person who has put in service feels recognised and puts forth his best on his promotion

2. Transfers:

Employees of the firm's other departments and non-selling section of sales department may also be considered for carer in sales department. The personnel department has the history of each employee potentially promising one can be considered by itrangers gives chance to others to come in.

3. Re-employment of former employees :

It is another source of excellence. In case of those candidates whose past records are elean and sound, can be called back to original work situations in case they are willing. There is no harm in employing past employees as they are seasoned and are sure to be loyal. Theyadd to the reputation o the firm without the costs of selection, training and turnover.

## MERITS AND DEMERITS OF INTERNAL SOURCES

**Merits :**

There are good many advantages or the benefits of falling back on the internal sources of recruitment. These are

1. High employee morale :

lt is but natural that an employee from within who has worked so sincerely and hard e expectssome evasion, recognition, praise, promotion or upgrading. If such a person's wish is considered it tells very nicely on his career and careers of others in the company and that of company itself where there will be sound employer employee relations.

2. Reduced costs of hiring:

Recruiting a candidate from external source is a costly affair in terms of time Even with much care being exercise recruiting, there is no guarantee that you would get a really good hand therefore, the statement "known enemy is better than an unknown friend that works

3. No training:

   A new candidate recruited and selected needs a thorough training as he is a raw-hand training. Costs in terms of time, talent and treasure. However, in case of an in house candidate there is no no need for special training. Nor there will be any problem of placement because the old guy are self starter

4. No transitory loss:

   It takes longer time to fill in the vacancies from outside sources. a new candidate is to be recruited , selected, trained and place. As he is new, he takes time adjust himself to work situation or atmosphere, to build confidence. In this, is the firm that suffers in form ofloss of sales, outside contacts and position in market places.

5. Assured loyalty:

   In case internal employees are considered for the post they tend to be more sincere Honest and hard working as they develop a sense of belonging They know that sooner or later everyone stand a chance of up gradation

**Demerits:**

1. Diacord

   In case there are limited sets to be filled and many are craving for the posts, may lead unfair means to grab that position in the organization it means merit and performance have no place. The result in heart burning jealousy and frustration. The organization may be divided into blocks fighting among themselves

2. Prerogative:

   If the firm follows this policy of internal promotion or considering the cases for vacant Post employees feels it is a matter of their right. This puts the management in difficulties because, there will be no chance for new blood coming in at all.

*What are the external sources of recruitment?*

1. Advertising in newspapers and periodicals is one of the most important methods ot recruitment. This is specially so in case of recruitment of management and technical personnel. The company needing manpower advertises details about the job, requirements, salary perquisites, duties and responsibilities etc. The advantage of advertising is that all details about the job can be given in advertisement to allow self-screening by the prospective candidates. Advertisement gives the management a wider range of candidates from which to choose. Its disadvantage is that it brings large number of applications whose screening costs may be quite heavy.
2. Employment Agencies: There are government as well as private employment agencies providing a nation-wide or area-wise service in matching personnel demand and supply. In India, there are employment exchanges and employment and guidance bureau which provide a range of service. In some cases, compulsory notification of vacancies to the employment exchange is required by law. Employment seekers get themselves registered with these exchanges. The employment exchanges bring the job-givers in contact with job-seekers. Employment exchanges are well regarded particularly in the field of unskilled, semi-skilled and skilled operative jobs. However, in the technical and professional area, private consultancy firms provide recruitment facilities. In metropolitan cities, there are several such agencies prominent among them are Tata Consultancy Service, A.F. Ferguson and Company, ABS Consultants etc.
3. Gate Hiring: In a country like ours, where there is a large number of unemployed people, it is usual to find job-seekers thronging the factory gates. Whenever workers are required, the people who are available at the gate, are recruited in necessary number. This method can be used safely for unskilled workers. In some industries, a large number of workers work as badli or substitute workers. Whenever a permanent worker is absent, a

substitute is employed in his place from among the people at the gate.

4. Educational Institution: Direct recruitment from colleges and universities is prevalent for the recruitment of higher staff in western countries but not in India. Many big organisations maintain a close liaison with educational institutions for recruitment to various jobs. Various recruiting groups develop systematic formal university recruiting programmes. They hold preliminary on-campus interviews and select some students for final interview mostly at their offices.
5. Employee recommendations-In order to encourage existing employees, some concern have made a policy to recruit further staff only from the applicants introduced and recommended by employees or employees' union. Other conditions being equal, preference will be given to friends and relatives of existing employees.
6. Labour Unions-In many organisations, labour unions are regarded as a source from which to recruit manpower. This facilitates increasing the sense of cooperation and in developing the better industrial relations. But sometimes trade unions support a candidate who is not suitable for the job and not acceptable to management. This weakens the labour relations.
7. Leasing: To adjust short term fluctuations in personnel needs, the possibilities of leasing personnel for some specified period may be considered. This system of leasing has been v. ell adopted by the public sector organisations with the rapid growth of public sector, the acute shortage of managerial personnel has been solved by borrowing the personnel from the Government departments. At the end of their term they are given option to choose either parent services or the present organisation.
8. Waiting Lists-Many organisations prepare waiting lists of candidates who have gone through the recruitment processes but who have not been employed for the time being. When the need arises, such candidates may be called for employment.

Such a source can be developed through provisions of attractive employment.

9. Field Trips-At interviewing team makes trips to towns and tides which are known to contain the kinds of employees required by the enterprise. Arrival dates and the time and venue of interview are advertised in advance.

10. Unsolicited Applications: One of the important source of recruitment is unsolicited applicants who send their requests for appointment against a vacancy, if any. By appointing such casual callers the employer saves not only the selection and training costs but also expenditure in the form of pension, insurance and fringe benefits.

11. Labour Contractors:In many Indian industries, workers are recruited through contractors who are themselves the employees of these organisation.

12. Ex-employee's: Ex-employee means persons who have even worked in the enterprise and have left the organisation and now eager to return. Such employees having good record may be preferred. They will require less initial training.

## SELECTION

The process of interviewing and evaluating candidates for a specific job and selecting an individual for employment based on certain criteria. Employee selection can range from a very simple process to a very complicated process depending on the firm hiring and the position. Certain employment laws such as anti-discrimination laws must be obeyed during employee selection.

## STANDARD DEFINITIONS

Professor Dale Yoder:

Selection is the process in which candidate for employment are divide into two classes those who are offered employment and those who are not

Professor Dale S. Beach:

"Whereas the goal of recruitment is to create large pool of persons who are available and willing to work" the selection process has its objective of sorting outor eliminating of those judged unqualified to meet job and

## SIGNIFICANCE OF SOUND SELECTION

The hard nut to crack is that of selecting the competent salesmen. Intelligent selectionof sales personnel is a critical and crucial matter for the fortunes of the business and businesshouse depends on the quality of sales force performance. The importance of sound selection is reflected in the following points

1. It lowers the rate of turnover of sales force:

   The experience of many large concerns has demonstrated very clearly that sound selectionis the cause of lower sales force turnover and increased sales. Faulty selection on semi-baked ideas Costs high more turnover means more hiringand training costs as the firm indulges this year., the turnover has psychological impact on the customers and prospects and co-salesmen. The sales turnover also suffers during transitory period.

2. Inefficiency is curbed:

   Poor selection policies and procedure percolate the poor, ineffective and inefficient Salesman to the bottom of the organisation. These mediocre salesmen show marks of dwindling Sales increasing expenses very soon as they are far below the level of competency. A salesman without qualification experience, confidence and proficiency, is neither happy himself nor allows others to be happy. It affects the working culture and morale of other workers very badly so much so that even the horses turn to be donkeys-

3. Solves sales administration problems:

   In addition to reducing the turnover of salesmen and decreasing the costs of selection and training, a good selection programme

Simplifies traiņing problem, improves supervision, ensures better territory coverage and service to the customers attracts better class of recruits, forestall un ionstation and above all, simplifies salesmen control in the interest of the sales organisation.

## METHODS OF SELECTION

There cannot be one method or a plan of selecting the salesmen for all the sales organisations.lt is obvious that each sales organisation enjoys a unique position caught in its own environment. The selection methods or procedures or plans differ widely from company to company in view Of the individual differences in size, nature of products sold, location, status in labour and money markets, characteristics and philosophies of management However forthe sake of convenience these methods can be broadly of two types namely inductive and deductive _ Let us consider these in brief as to what are their implications.

I. Inductive method

It is that Selection procedure under which a study is made of most successful salesmen inthe past .A selected number is defined .the team studies the qualities that brought them to such a glittering success.The listed Qualities' are used as a test to see whether the new recruitsare possessing these though it is a good idea it takes into account those qualities The success in the past. lt is wrong to say that Mr. 'X' succeeded in past so Mr. 'Y' to shouldsucceed in future This expected success is situational. This leads to wrong conclusions that is why, this method is not widely

Il. Deductive method:

This method works on different lines. It undertakes a detailed study of salesman's job its knowledge and analyses it. In other words, it starts with job analysis. It also analysis the personal history of present salesmen in the organisation. Based on these standard qualifications or qualities are determined for different types of salesman. Then efforts are made to measure to what extent the candidate fulfils these through various stages or technique of selection as application, interview, reference testing, and so on. Thus, this deductive most commonly employed.

## SELECTION PROCESS

1. Preliminary Interviews- It is used to eliminate those candidates who do not meet the minimum eligiblity criteria laid down by the organization. The skills, academic and family background, competencies and interests of the candidate are examined during preliminary interview. Preliminary interviews are less formalized and planned than the final interviews. The candidates are given a brief up about the company and the job profile; and it is also examined how much the candidate knows about the company. Preliminary interviews are also called screening interviews.
2. Application blanks- The candidates who clear the preliminary interview are required to fill application blank. It contains data record of the candidates such as details about age, qualifications, reason for leaving previous job, experience, etc.
3. Written Tests- Various written tests conducted during selection procedure are aptitude test, intelligence test, reasoning test, personality test, etc. These tests are used to objectively assess the potential candidate. They should not be biased.
4. Employment Interviews- It is a one to one interaction between the interviewer and the potential candidate. It is used to find whether the candidate is best suited for the required job or not. But such interviews consume time and money both. Moreover the competencies of the candidate cannot be judged. Such interviews may be biased at times. Such interviews should be conducted properly. No distractions should be there in room. There should be an honest communication between candidate and interviewer.
5. Medical examination- Medical tests are conducted to ensure physical fitness of the potential employee. It will decrease chances of employee absenteeism.

6. Appointment Letter- A reference check is made about the candidate selected and then finally he is appointed by giving a formal appointment letter.

*Realistic job previews*

Methods like this are time-consuming and there are serious issues of confidentiality, but if you can screen your shortlist down to two or three candidates, there's no reason why you shouldn't bring them in and give them a problem to handle.

You do need to make sure that the problem has a clear solution; preferably, it would be a problem that you've already dealt with successfully.

A benefit with realistic job previews is that they can involve more staff in the selection procedure. People tend to work well with candidates whom they have seen and had some say about.

*Portfolios*

Portfolios are little used in the United Kingdom with the exception of specialist professions, such as photography or graphic design. However, the development of portfolios such as Records of Achievement seems to indicate that this may be changing.

## REFERENCES

Written references have some drawbacks; perhaps someone wants rid of an employee - they certainly won't give a poor reference under those circumstances! Poor references could also turn out to be libellous, although one of the main problems is that people just don't know what you're asking for. The most accurate references may come from face-to-face or telephone interviews with someone who has had direct experience of the candidate's work.

If you're writing, you could ask for a telephoned reply or say that you will telephone them. Where this isn't possible, enclose a copy of the information that you have collected about the job and ask the referee if the candidate is suitable for this job. To get the best response, allow a decent length of time for reply and do not send a massive form for the referee to complete.

### *Assessment centres*

An assessment centre will put candidates through a series of tests, exercises and perhaps interviews, lasting, typically, a day. Candidates are observed by a team of assessors, with others acting as facilitators. Tests and exercises are used which are designed to predict how candidates will perform in the workplace. Realistic job previews, lateral thinking exercises, psychometric tests and practical demonstrations are all popular events in an assessment centre.

Care must be given to select tests that will draw out appropriate skills, knowledge and ability, and assessment must be weighted so demonstration of more desirable attributes wins more 'points' than those that are 'nice to have' but not essential.

### *Other methods*

Perhaps the most popular of the other methods available is psychometric testing, which offers actual tests in areas such as intelligence and personality characteristics. These include Raymond Cattell's 16 PF Test, which broadly demonstrates candidates' emotional stability. The Myers Briggs Test is reasonably user-friendly (it's short) and purports to identify people by personality characteristics such as extrovert v. introvert and thinking vs feeling.

Finally, there are selection methods which use samples of candidates' handwriting (graphology), their star sign (astrology) or which select through palmistry. Little evidence exists to support these as adequate predictors of performance.

What is important is to know what you want and to use processes with which you feel comfortable in order to select your candidate.

# SALES FORCE MOTIVATION

## LEARNING OBJECTIVES:

An enthusiastic and motivated sales force is the best possible foundation for successful achievement of sales objectives. This topic should help you understand:

- That the definition of motivation includes the motivational mix and all of its various elements.
- The powerful motivating influence of a high-performance sales culture.
- The importance of realizing that salespeople have basic needs that, when met are strongly motivating.
- The model for a salesperson?s behavior.
- The benefit of knowing salespeople personally.
- That not every member of a sales force can be motivated.

## BACKGROUND

A successful sales manager is one who earns the enthusiasm, loyalty and interest of sales- force which cannot be bought for a price. This earning depends upon the ability to motivate sales-force. It is because; there can be vast difference in sales volume produced by individual salesman with equal qualifications, opportunity and training. A salesman sells more for his sales manager who earns his confidence and whole-hearted effort through skillful motivation. A motive is an idea, need, or an emotion within an individual which incites him to action. It can aroused by some external influence or incentive or stimuli.

## SOME DEFINATIONS OF SALES-FORCE MOTIVATION

D.E. McFarland, "Motivation relates those forces operating within the individual employee or subordinate which compel him to act or not to act in certain ways."

Stanley Vance, "Motivation implies any emotion or desire which so conditions one?s will that individual is propelled into action."

Berson, "Motivation is an inner state that energizes, activates or moves or channelizes behavior towards goal."

Prof. William G. Scott, "Motivation means a process of stimulating people to accomplish desired goals."

Motivation is a psychological set of forces influencing the behavior of an individual. It is the willingness to expand energy to achieve goal or reward. To motivate sales-force, a sales manager is expected to know the needs and emotions of his salesmen; its emotional, mental and physical needs. In essence, motivation is linked with will to work. It is act of changing the psychology of a salesman to make him to work better; it is the task of intensifying the desire to work at one?s higher pitch, it is to encourage, stimulate, and elevate to lift up productivity.

## IMPORTANCE OF MOTIVATION

Sales organizations are made of human beings working at different levels and every organization needs people in order to function. Motivation in itself is a highly complex activity & affected by large numbers of the factors in organization. Employees in an organization possess a huge amount of information based on the experiences about the structures & processes of the sales organization and market. Sales organizations serve as resource pool & talent. The success of a sales organization depends on the ability and the style of the functioning of the sales manager to motivate the sale staff.

They get de-motivated due to:

- Frequent rejections by customers,
- Lower esteem
- Customer complaints
- Nature of the job
- Frequent travelling

***The Process of Motivation:***

The sales manager need to understand the process of motivation & uses it to improve firm?s efficiency. He can use this to stimulate sales person to work efficiently. This starts when a motive prompts people to action. Motives are the primary energizer of behavior. Motives are largely subjective and represent the mental picture of the salesperson. They arise continuously and determine the general direction of the salesperson?s behavior.

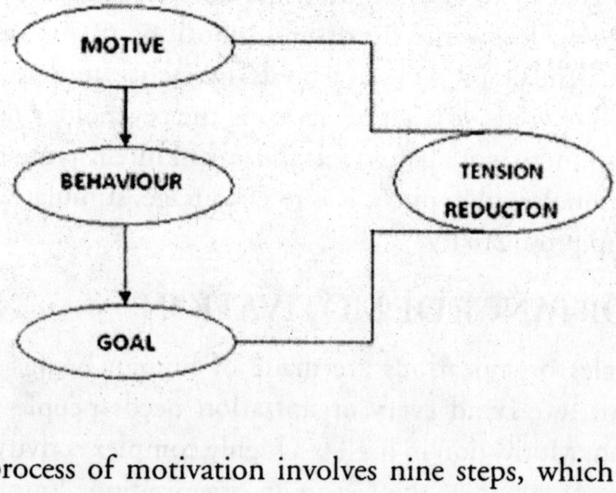


The process of motivation involves nine steps, which are as follows:

1. Determination of objective:

   It is essential to determine at this stage on which reasons, the salesman are to be motivated. When the objectives are determined, it will be easier to ascertain the levels, resources and the methods of motivation. It is because; the idea is to get the very best out of every sales person.

2. Studying the needs of sales-people:

   Once the sales manager determines the objectives, the managers should take steps to study the sentiments and the needs of the sales people to select the motivators that are to be used for motivating them on specific occasions. This necessitates the study of individual differences between persons, their mental conditions, positions, the post they hold.

3. Determination of motivational tools:

   Keeping in view the place of working, duration and working hours and timings, the society they belong and their needs, alternate tools are developed. While deciding the motivational tools, attention is paid to the financial conditions of the enterprise. The tools that are selected should project the needs of the specific individuals or of the group, and they should be the best alternative to satisfy the needs of the sales people.

4. Communication of motivational plan:

   For any motivational plan to be successful, it is to be sold to the beneficiaries by finest means of communication. Each sales-person covered under the plan, should know the ins and outs of the plan, the benefits they get, the way it is calculated,

5. Integrating diverse interests:

   The expectations and the expectation levels differ from individual to individual as employees and as opposed to this, the organizational expectations also differ. In case, both ends do not meet, there will be conflicts. That is why; there is great need of integration of interests of employees and the organization.

6. Selection and application of suitable motivators:

   It is not the question of motivating factors or motivators but particular selected blend of motivators is important. A motivator may be very good, yet it may not be suitable. Suitability is more important, just like viability is more important than liability.

7. Creation of auxiliary environment:

   Working conditions, both physical and mental, are important in motivating sales people. In this regard, auxiliary environment may be created within the organization by providing various ways and means for the individual development through training of right sort.

8. Developing team spirit:

   Development of team spirit is an important step towards the dizzy height of sound motivational process. This stupendous task calls for identification and realization of importance to individuals. Individuals as individuals are important because they have tremendous potential for achievement provided they join their hands. It is rightly said, "United We Stand Divided We Fall". Therefore, individual efforts should be directed towards achieving institutional objectives, which would be possible by developing and inculcating the significance and hidden strength of team spirit among the sales-people so that they may function as the members of the team.

9. Feedback arrangement:

   Feedback or follow-up is the last step in the process of motivation. At this stage, the results are compared as against the motivational plans designed as implemented. The gaps between the actual and the planned performance can be gauged, causes are found out and the necessary changes can be performed in the weak areas.

## PRINCIPLES OF MOTIVATION

The thing about motivation is that to get better results from the psychological of function, certain principles that are given or stated by the experts in the field of motivation should be taken care of and respected. These principles guide how one can motivate its employees and sales person to get the best of it.

1. Principle of feeling of security:

   A motivation programme should have the quality of developing a feeling of security among the sales people. If the employee feels secured about his job, he is satisfied with his job, a long tenure with the company and a chance to grow and make a career.

2. Principle of Achievement:

   The employee has his goals and targets that he sets for himself he thus needs motivation to work towards achieving those targets which will give the employee a feeling of achievement and he will be self motivated for achieving future goals.

3. Principle of praise and approval:

   The common notion that others should not be praised and approved as it can be taken in a negative way. But the work done by the employees in good way should be praises by the approved in front of everyone so that others get motivated to work to be praised in everybody.

4. Principle of respect and loyalty:

   the employee becomes loyal to the company when he feels a sense of belonging to the company, the company when gives the employee a sense of belonging then the employee becomes loyal to the company and respects all the sub ordinates , seniors respect the juniors and vice versa. This creates a healthy environment on the company and they feel what is good for the company is also good for them.

5. Principle of advancement:

   Every employee in a company wants to advance in the company to higher positions. All the employees deserve equal rights to advance and thus they should be provided too. The employees thus get motivated and work hard for the company to get their right to advance in the company.

6. Principle of leadership:

   The seniors in a company become role models for juniors and they try to work in a way that try to work to become like them and thus they unknowingly motivate them to work hard for the company and follow in the footsteps of their leaders.

7. Principle of spiritual, moral and social ideology respect:

   The seniors in a company have to motivate its workers and the work force to work for the betterment of the company. The juniors should be morally motivated to follow the morals of the company to raise the spirits of the employees and follow the social ideology of the company ethics.

8. Principle of participation:

   A good manager has to make all his sub ordinates involve in all the activities of the company so that they can find out their strengths and weaknesses and thus work towards them and motivate them to work on improving them. The participation make the employee motivated towards taking initiation in future activities of the company.

9. Principle of team spirit:

   a company is not run by one person, or a project is not worked upon by a single person, it has to be done in a team thus a manager has to make all his employees work in a team and sometimes they have to be motivated to work In a team even though they have problems in working as a team.

10. Principle of existence:

    The employees want to be noticed in their workplace, they want everybody to notice them and their work in their company. If the work of an employee is appreciated by others and his work and his existence is given importance then he gets motivated towards improving and growing with his work.

11. Principle of surfacing hidden abilities:

    Every person has his own sets of skills which includes their abilities to complete tasks, their techniques, knowledge which is all different to the ones possessed by others. They should be motivated by their manager to explore the skills that they are not aware about by involving them in team activities which are specially devised to help employees explore their skills and improve them.

## FACTORS AFFECTING MOTIVATION OF SALES-FORCE:

Before motivating the sales-force, the sales manager is to have a thorough understanding of the motives, impulses or urges behind the work. He should identify the forces that motivates salesmen to gear up to productive effort, company loyalty and enthusiasm what makes them to put their heart and soul together. The worldwide studies reveal certain motives which are most significant behind a marked performance, and these are as follows:

1. Recognition And Praise:

   Salesmen seek recognition for their achievements and praise for the work done which they think is more than monetary gain for them. The common complaint of sales-force is that sales managers rarely praise their work. Failure to compliment and praise is ignoring a vital need in salesman?s nature having deeper impact on sales performance.

2. Fair Pay Packet:

   Though financial incentives are secondary to recognition and praise, it is dormant motive because salesman is to earn a decent living for himself and his dependents. It is but natural that he expects an assurance of salary that is comparable with his collogues in his own organization and competitive organization with equal performance and responsibilities. Therefore it should be attractive and assured one.

3. Good Working Conditions:

   It is the working conditions- both physical and psychological that influence his attitude towards his work and performance. Thus, a salesman looks for a territory that gives him adequate sales potential, he expects a fair division of compensation on all joint sales efforts. He is likely to accept an adequate and regular expense allowance. The other such conditions may be freedom from excessive paperwork, cozy of his facilities, feeling of home away from home and so on.

4. Opportunity For Advancement:

   Many sales people give top priority to promotion to hire ups than to attractive salary or even job security. By nature, he does not want to be stagnant. Any company that fails to provide such an opportunity for advancement will be responsible for high sale-force turnover by depriving the basic need and creating dissatisfaction and injecting frustration.

5. Good Supervision And Leadership:

   The productivity of sales-force is dependent on the very nature of leadership provided in the company from sale manager down up to sales supervisors. Every manager is a leader and not a boss. Salesmen look at their superior as outstanding in terms of industry, knowledge. Salesmen respect those who are fair and impartial, determined, keep words, accommodate the personal dignity of salesmen they expect that their leaders should understand them, their problems and solve them.

6. Opportunity For Self-Expression:

   Salesmen have their own views, attitudes, suggestions, ideas, which they want to express, assert their personalities and exploit their latest talents and abilities. A salesman is sure to increase his sales effort if he has the opportunity to assert himself, express his personality. Absence and suppression of salesman?s expression and assertion will kill his initiative, drive and enthusiasm. Management stands benefited by such rich services of untapped source of new ideas to increasing sales, cutting down costs and improving profitability.

7. Social Acceptance:

   Every human-being- a social and rational animal- has the strong feeling of "belonging? to the group. Salesmen naturally desire the acceptance goodwill of their association in business. It is the sales manager?s task to develop a sense of "belongingness" in case of every salesman. He wants to have the satisfaction of being accepted as a member of a sales team, sales organization, having his actual participation, voice in its affairs, cooperating in matters of mutual interest.

8. Job Security:

Every salesman expects he has job security. That is, he will be able to retain his job as long as his work is quite satisfactory and the prevailing economic and social conditions permit. Job security does not mean absolute performance of job tenure. He means - protection from arbitrary discharge or dismissal or transfer. Salary is not the only factor that determines such security. He looks to future social security. When he gets old, he should have the opportunities of reasonable earnings to pull on longer with respect and dignity.

9. Desire To Excel:

One finds the strong urge of excelling others in performance and achievement. It speaks of aggressiveness of any successful salesmen. Desire to excel others implies increasing sales, cutting costs, improving profitability. It is a motive that helps both the parties in that the management can prosper and that prosperity is made to share by the sales-force.

1o. Pride In Selling:

Job satisfaction is another strong motive of every salesman. This job satisfaction is dependent on pride in selling as a vocation. When one has accepted a sales career, it should not be looked down upon. The salesman should not have a feeling that he is doing some worthless job to hang on or as a matter of last resort or as a means of livelihood. Therefore, the significance of selling must be emphasized in preparing and training salesmen. They should be given an understanding that they are doing creative, gainful, socially acceptable and respected job.

## METHODS OF MOTIVATION:

Method 1 of 2: Improving Sales Environments

1. Schedule meetings with your sales staff regularly:

Instead of focusing on what they are doing wrong, make sure

that some 1-on-1 meetings address their worries, pain points and work environment issues. You are likely to catch motivation problems before they affect their season and quota, if you try to fix negative work pressures.

Ask your sales staff what motivates them during these meetings. You may find some salespeople respond to monetary rewards, while others respond to promotions or a supportive team environment. Take notes on what motivates each person.

2. Train your salespeople.

   There are several ways to plan trainings to increase motivation:

a. Appoint salespeople to train their peers. This is an excellent way to recognize special skills in your salespeople and encourage interaction. Ask the salesperson to take a few hours from selling and plan a 1-hour training session about a topic they excel in.

b. Take a field trip. Use your contacts to find a manager who would be willing to have you watch their successful sales team. Consider making the place a sales floor for a different product or industry. For example, if your sales team needs to be more aggressive, take them to a conference where they can witness someone selling a product with a 30-second elevator speech. Return and ask them to write a new introduction speech.

c. Choose an outside consultant to train your salespeople. Pick your person very carefully. Make sure they are an expert, they have excellent time management skills and they are able to inject some humor into the training. Keep training sessions short and include a practice period with the guest speaker.

d. Appoint a mentor to train younger sales associates. This may help the younger staff work through the growing pains of a new job. Give the mentors incentives if the younger associates meet their sales goals. This is a great option for a workplace that requires team building.

3. Invest in new sales tools:

   Make sure your CRM is enhancing the sales environment, rather than detracting from it. A good reporting, mass email or mobile app tool can increase a salesperson's efficiency, helping their sales goals and their motivation.

Most new websites and CRM require a training period. They can be easier for some salespeople to learn than others. Time the adoption of the tool to a low-stress point in the season.

Method 2 of 2: Motivational Strategies:

1. Tailor your motivational plan to each employee:

   If you have the ability to adjust incentive schemes, use it. Each person is motivated differently, so choose 1 to 3 things that will help the salesperson work harder and put them in writing.

2. Create a reasonable and effective commission structure:

   If few of your salespeople are meeting their quotas, you should review how well they are working to motivate employees. Reconsider caps on commissions or quotas, placing them at lower levels if the market has seen a drop or raising the commission levels in a market boom.

3. Implement daily, weekly and monthly incentives:

   Offering a trip, day off, large gift card, coffee, free lunches or gym/club membership for the most sales in a week will encourage staff to go the extra mile. These interim bonuses can also help salespeople to meet their larger quotas by helping them hit milestones during the season.

   Incentives also increase friendly competition. Competing on a daily basis for new leads or lead qualification can cause people to push each other to do better. Keep incentives at a value where they increase friendly competition but do not encourage sabotage.

4. Create a personal goal:

   Keeping in mind what motivates each employee, tack on an incentive to their commission that applies to their desires. For example, if you know an employee has an anniversary, offer them 2 extra paid days of leave if they meet their goal.

5. Encourage a team environment:

   Salespeople can often feel like they are alone, working toward a target. Create a team incentive where they are encouraged to help each other and share knowledge for a common goal.

6. Recognize sales achievements:

   The time you take to congratulate someone on their hard work may decide how hard they work to reach their next quota. Consider these recognition strategies. Congratulate them publicly. Bring up their achievement at sales meetings. Be as specific as possible with the details of their success. For example, say "Joe's ability to obtain referrals is exceptional. He has the highest referral rate in the company, which leads to him hitting his quotas. Joe can you tell us how you ask someone to refer you to their friends and associates? Write the person a note. Do not wait until their yearly review to give them recognition. Instead, send a letter to their house to tell them how valued they are, with a gift card for their family. Introduce the person and their achievements to your bosses. Recognition in upper management is hard to get, especially if your sales staff sees high turnover. When someone surpasses goals, schedule meetings where they can meet with higher staff or invite them to sit in on a strategy meeting.

## REFERENCES

1. www.wikipedia.com
2. www.slideshare.com
3. www.wikihow.com
4. Advertising and Sales Management by Sontakki
5. Sales Management by Charles M. Futrell
6. www.flexstudy.com
7. www.executiveblueprints.com
8. www.psychologytoday.com

# SALES-FORCE TRAINING ORIENTATION AND PLACEMENT

## SALES TRAINING

## INTRODUCTION

The training of sales team subordinates is a fundamental responsibility of the sales manager. He or she can delegate that responsibility to a sales training manager or to individual field sales line managers, each of whom is accountable for the performance of their direct subordinate team. But the company sales manager cannot abdicate the sales training responsibility.

The purpose of training is to improve the overall competence of members of a sales team, and this is usually tackled by sales managers working to:

- impart knowledge of the company, its products, and its markets
- create or change attitudes that affect performance
- develop skills that increase performance
- develop habits that contribute to improved performance
- reduce the level of field management supervision subsequently needed
- increase job satisfaction (reducing sales force turnover).

## SALES TRAINING

Sales training may be defined as those things which are done to help salespeople gain mastery in the skills, concepts, behaviors, and attitudes that will enhance their expertise in influencing prospects to make positive purchasing decisions. Sales training concentrates on how prospective sellers and buyers interact. It provides tools and techniques that help salespeople learn what they must know in order to persuasively present their goods or services to buyers in terms that buyers will understand and ultimately respond to.

According to Mr G.R.Collins, "Sales training is an organized activity involving fact finding, planning, coaching, practicing and positive attempt to develop selling skill and add these skills to selected native ability casually acquired knowledge and experience".

## SIGNIFICANCE OF SALES TRAINING

It was considered that salesmen were 'born 'and are not 'made' due to which training was considered a futile exercise. The need for training arises due to following reasons:

- To better the sales performance- It means to increase the sales volume, decreasing the selling costs and increasing the profits through improved productivity and profitability. Sales performance can be better through sales training only.
- To provide expert knowledge-There is no substitute available for actual experience that is gained not bought. It is the sales training that briefs, cuts, shapes, polishes and prunes the novice to acquire essential knowledge about his products, people himself so that he can come up in sales box with confidence and guarantee.
- To curb wastages in the unit-A well trained salesman is sure to cause least amount of waste of time, talent and treasure. The rate of turnover is reduced to great extent as the firm is blessed with a satisfied salesman.
- To influence the people favorably-It teaches the best ways to influence the people dealing with fastidious customers, handling, complaints, opening new accounts, negotiating at top and obtaining sales appointments, planning the growing

and diversifying work, preparing quotations and talks and closing the sales.

- To improve his earnings-Effective sales training results in increase of sales and earnings to win recognition and to qualify for promotion to a supervisory position of salesman attitude and interests, this greatly changes and improves the work.
- To sweeten the employer employee relationship-Salesman with self confidence and responsible nature is a contented soul with rich and scientific training. So long the employer employee relations are sound and sweet no force on earth will damage the organizational growth and prospects.

## LIMITATIONS OF SALES TRAINING

There are certain limitations which are caused due to sales manager and do not impart training to salesman are as follows:

- It is expensive-Training to Salesman is a costly affair and the range is from Rs 25,000 to Rs 65,000 depending on the complexity of the sales job. It includes training period material, salary, instructions, and time. At any time, the trainee may be flicked by competitors.
- It is time consuming-Many employers hesitate to train their sales army because f the prolonged time for completing the training programme. The usual time narrated by a sound training programme varies widely depending on the complexity of sales task and nature of products sold.
- Results are intangible and slow-The Salesman who is more experienced in a line is superior to new man. There is no substitute for such rich and varied experience. This tangle makes the firms to go in for the sales training. Therefore, the employers accept the proposal with two minds because the results are not really tangible and slow in impact.
- It turns spasmodic and conflicting-Some managers think that selling involves good many variables and is not possible to train a person to deal with complex sales situations. Therefore, the

training must be well organized, planned, continuous and implemented failing which other sales problems side-track this training making it spasmodic and conflicting finally resulted in a failure.

However plus points out weigh the minus points and make a very strong care for the sales training.

## OBJECTIVE OF SALES TRAINING

The objectives are as follows-

- To acquaint the new recruits with the fundamentals of successful selling.
- To reduce the turnover and absenteeism of sales-force.
- To improve the productivity and proficiency of professional selling.
- To build a reserve-force to replace those who vacate at any moment of time.
- To identify and cull the misfits from the organizations.
- To raise the employee morale for sound men and boss relations.

## AREAS OF SALES TRAINING

Sales training is very important and comprehensive phrase and divided into the knowledge, skill and attitude.

Sales Knowledge:

- Company knowledge.
- The sales role.
- Product knowledge.
- Prices.
- Advertising and sales promotion.
- Channels of distribution.
- Customers.
- Competition, industry, and economy.
- Territorial management skills.

Product Knowledge:

Product knowledge may include these technical details:

- Performance data.
- Physical size and characteristics.
- How the product operates.
- Specific product features, advantages, and benefits.
- How well the product is selling in the marketplace.

Channels or Distribution:

Some important information salespeople need includes:

- The likes and dislikes of each channel member's customers.
- The product lines and assortment each one carries.
- When each member sees salespeople.
- Each member's distribution, promotional, and pricing policies.
- What and how much of a product each has purchased in the past.

*Sales Skill Development:*

Involves two key elements:

1. Persuasive communications.
2. The selling process

Several main persuasive communication skills are:

- Talking about product benefits to the prospect rather than the product's features and advantages.
- Nonverbal body language - learning to recognize a buyer's nonverbal signs and how to send out positive nonverbal body signals.
- Questioning or probing skills and courses in listening.
- Using visual aids, drama, and demonstrations in the sales presentation.

## PLANNING AND DESIGNING SALES TRAINING PROGRAMME

There are good number and types of sales training programs.

The tasks of planning and designing the sales training program which is comprehensive, purposive, and productive and result oriented.

**Decision one**

- ACCESS
- Need to Know: Want training delivered when they need it, when ready to progress to a new task or next stage.
- Self Concept: Desire to be recognized by instructor as independent and self-directed.
- Life Experience: Expect instructor to recognize their prior accomplishments and knowledge.
- Task-centered and Practical: Training should help them meet job-related needs.
- Internally Motivated: Largely (but not exclusively) driven by internal rewards and not, for example, grades or parental approval

Decision Two

- DESIGN

**Learning Outcomes**

- Attitudinal Learning: Outcomes that aim to change or enhance a learner's attitude or motivation about a subject
- Cognitive Learning: Outcomes that aim to contribute to a learner's body of knowledge about a topic.
- Skill Learning: Outcomes that aim to help a learner perform a job-related, behavioral task.

**Decision Three**

- DEVELOP

**Developing Learning**

- Develop learning experiences based on a specific learning outcome.
- The learning experience should be appropriate for accomplishing the learning outcome.

- The learning experience should be appropriate to the learning domain.
- Use a variety of learning experiences.
- Allow for questions and student-to-student interaction in each learning experience.
- Consider constraints in facilitating each learning experience

**Decision Four**

- IMPLEMENT

**Engaging learners**

- Ask learners what they want to learn from the training, and then list them.
- Probe learners with questions frequently; interactivity should be an primary characteristic of the training.
- Encourage application of material by providing examples, posing job-based problems, and asking learners to consider how they might apply what they are learning.
- Quiz and give feedback in a nonthreatening way.
- Pose alternative, thought-provoking questions and scenarios to get students to critique and question and get beyond the obvious.
- Start with what learners know to empower them and identify what to build on.
- Use both visual and aural (hearing) modes of learning.
- Use organizing that help learners keep track of where they are and what they've learned.
- Use humor and stories to enhance content and maintain learner motivation.

**Decision Five**

- EVALUATE

Evaluation of training can be separated into two primary categories:

- Formative: Occurs while the training is being designed, developed, and delivered. Allows trainers to determine what needs to change in their training plans and delivery.
- Summative: Usually completed immediately after training is conducted to evaluate the extent to which learners enjoyed and believed they received valuable learning. Can also be conducted over the course of weeks or months after training.

There is scope for improvement for the very best can be improved upon.

## PRINCIPLES OF SALES TRAINING-

1. Sales Process Alignment- Without a thorough understanding of the sales process (or processes) that enables your salespeople to align with buyers and close business, it is not possible to determine the types of competencies required for successful selling. As a result, most training initiatives omit critical training requirements completely. In addition, a sales process map also provides insight into sales tools and templates that provide the most impact for successful selling.
2. Objective Assessment and Measurement - Sales organizations need defined models for evaluating the knowledge and skills of sales professionals and managers. Without objective assessment and measurement, it is impossible to determine where gaps exist and how training investments impact the skills and abilities of the sales organization.
3. Realistic Training Plans- Training plans need to be layered over time, from basic concepts to more complex topics. Attempting to force too much learning content into a compressed timeframe is unrealistic, and yields little performance improvement. Role-based curriculum plans should lay out realistic, staged learning and reinforcement paths for salespeople and managers.
4. Comprehensive Curriculum- Many sales training initiatives focus on a single aspect of selling, such as opportunity management, and do not address many important competencies

(e.g., targeting, account planning, accessing power, etc.) The "learning library" needs to comprehensively span sales planning, execution, and management disciplines. As salespeople acquire core selling competencies, they should progressively have access to curriculum "dial-ups" that lead to mastery in advanced selling skills, such as negotiation, selling to executives, value selling, etc.

5. A Two -Tiered Reinforcement Model- Reinforcement needs to be both scheduled and On-demand. Many organizations provide on-demand learning and reinforcement assets that Receive limited usage, because salespeople and their managers are preoccupied with daily activity. Like other learners, salespeople need structured reinforcement that is aligned with their learning path, and "pushed" to the salesperson on a planned basis. On-demand assets provide a second tier of reinforcement that provide highly personalized access to content on an individual basis.

6. Repetition and Variety - Essential concepts need to be learned and reinforced in multiple forms across planned time horizons. Learning theory supports an ongoing learning experience that utilize multiple modalities. These forms of content delivery should both support the learning objective and offer variety to retain the interest of the learner. An effective program combines many forms of learning and reinforcement delivery, including instructor-led training, eLearning, virtual classrooms, "pushed" content, video sales scenarios, webcast "refresher" lessons, searchable knowledge repositories, and access to forums and discussions.

7. Scalable "Electronic Reinforcement System" (ERS) - Access to learning assets, essential How-to's, and sales tools need to be instantly accessible to salespeople in multiple forms. Salespeople should be able to quickly locate and access learning content through a number of logical pathways. These pathways can include a sales process map that links to learning content, a

searchable knowledge base, an indexed set of sales tools, direct linkage through CRM "playbooks," etc. When designed appropriately, these integrated assets comprise an "Electronic Reinforcement System" (ERS) that supports scalable reinforcement and self-coaching.

8. Unlimited Learning Access -The historical pricing model for sales training has been typically a cost "per-person, per-class." As a result, many aspects of useful intellectual property and methodology are not made available to the entire organization because of cost considerations. The consequences of this approach are that many useful areas of sales methodology are never addressed at any point in training initiatives. In our view, the program of the future provides open access to all methodological content, allowing teams and individuals to pursue unlimited learning opportunities.
9. On-the-Job Integration - CRM is used by a majority of sales organizations to organize and track opportunity related information. The "last mile" of learning and reinforcement can be accomplished by integrating essential how-to have and learning assets directly into CRM usage. These "playbooks" reinforce best practices and can also link to context-based learning resources that are focused on the actual task being undertaken.
10. Ongoing Program Management - Sales training programs need to be managed as a business investment. Quarterly business reviews (QBR's) that measure both learning and business metrics should be mandatory in any sales development program.

## METHODS OF TRAINING

Many methods of training are available- each has certain advantages and disadvantages. Here we list the different methods of training.

1. **Technology-Based Learning**

   Common methods of learning via technology include:

- Basic PC-based programs
- Interactive multimedia - using a PC-based CD-ROM
- Interactive video - using a computer in conjunction with a VCR
- Web-based training programs

The forms of training with technology are almost unlimited. A trainer also gets more of the learner's involvement than in any other environment and trainees have the benefit of learning at their own pace.

2. **On-The-Job Training**

Jumping right into work from day one can sometimes be the most effective type of training..

On-the-job training gives employees motivation to start the job. Some reports indicate that people learn more efficiently if they learn hands-on, rather than listening to an instructor. However, this method might not be for everyone, as it could be very stressful.

3. **Coaching/Mentoring**

Coaching/mentoring gives employees a chance to receive training one-on-one from an experienced professional. This usually takes place after another more formal process has taken place to expand on what trainees have already learned.

Here are three examples of coaching/mentoring:

Hire professional coaches for managers. Set up a formal mentoring program between senior and junior managers

Coaching/mentoring gives trainees the chance to ask questions and receive thorough and honest answers - something they might not receive in a classroom with a group of people.

4. **Lectures**

Lectures usually take place in a classroom-format. It seems the only advantage to a lecture is the ability to get a huge amount of information to a lot of people in a short amount of time. It has been said to be the least effective of all training methods. In many cases, lectures contain no form of interaction from the trainer to the trainee and can be quite boring. Studies show that people only retain 20 percent of what they are taught in a lecture.

5. **Group Discussions & Tutorials**

   These most likely take place in a classroom where a group of people discuss issues. For example, if an unfamiliar program is to be implemented, a group discussion on the new program would allow employees to ask questions and provide ideas on how the program would work best..

6. **Role Playing**

   Role playing allows employees to act out issues that could occur in the workplace. Key skills often touched upon are negotiating and teamwork. A role play could take place between two people simulating an issue that could arise in the workplace. This could occur with a group of people split into pairs, or whereby two people role play in front of the classroom.

   Role playing can be effective in connecting theory and practice, but may not be popular with people who don´t feel comfortable performing in front of a group of people.

7. **Case Studies**

   Case studies provide trainees with a chance to analyze and discuss real workplace issues. They develop analytical and problem-solving skills, and provide practical illustrations of principle or theory. Â They can also build a strong sense of teamwork as teams struggle together to make sense of a case.

All types of issues could be covered - i.e. how to handle a new product launch.

## GROUP TRAINING METHODS:

### *What is A Lecture?*

- When one person conveys information to a group by talking to them, with or without the use of visual aids, this is called a lecture.

- A formal lecture does not allow participation by the audience, and there is little or no interaction (or feedback) between the speaker and listeners.
- Lectures by the trainers or the branch managers to a group of say 15 to 25 salesmen is the most common method of group training.
- However, it is one of the way approaches where trainees are passive listeners or observers.

### *When Should Lectures Be Used?*

- A lecture is suitable for large groups where interaction is not practical.
- Lectures are appropriate when the material has little relevance to personal experiences (e.g. technical theory).

When a speaker is a recognized expert in a field of study, lectures are used because the audience is primarily there to hear what is being said.

ADVANTAGES:

- Lectures are an efficient use of time.
- Lectures allow experts to share information with large groups.
- The material in a lecture is consistent, and listeners are not side tracked by comments/questions from the audience.
- Doubts are cleared on the spot.
- Effective when audio-visual aids are used.

DRAWBACKS:

- The lecturer cannot be sure their message was correctly received by the audience, unless a separate discussion period is used for follow up.
- Often the overall depth of learning will be relatively low because there is limited interaction, but the lecture method is very popular in universities and many professional situations.
- The successful transfer of information is completely dependent upon the skills of the lecturer (essentially it is one way communication).

- Difficulty of evaluation.

### *What is a Demonstration?*

- When a trainer has the audience actually performs a task by showing and explaining how to do it, this is called a demonstration.
- During a demonstration, the audience is encouraged to ask questions and request assistance as they try to do the task by themselves.
- Under this method, the trainer shows the salesman or a group of salesmen how to present facts, meet competition, open interview, answer objections and conduct demonstrations.

### *When Should Demonstrations be Used?*

- The demonstration method is effective when teaching skills.
- Demonstrations are appropriate when there is plenty of time for interaction because practice is necessary to master most skills.

Demonstrations are best for small groups, or when adequate staff is available to work with a large group.

ADVANTAGES:

- Demonstrations provide a hands-on experience (hear, see, do).
- Participants have plenty of interaction with trainers, and everyone is allowed to progress at their own pace as they master the skill.
- Trainees gain practical insight.
- Develops physical insight.
- It is motivating as things are not dummy.

DRAWBACKS:

- Demonstrations require a lot of preparation, time, materials, and patience. The time allotted for demonstrations must be flexible.
- It is important to insure every participant has an opportunity to master the skill being taught.

- Hands-on activities can be a potential source of frustration, especially in the case of complex skills. It may be necessary to offer supplementary help (e.g. a follow-up session) for participants having difficulty.

### *What is a Discussion?*

- When a trainer guides an open conversation (an organized exchange of ideas or viewpoints) on a selected topic, this is called a discussion.
- A formal discussion (sometimes called a panel) follows a set procedure that is used to keep the discussion on track, and allows everyone to express their opinion.

### *When Should Discussions be Used?*

- Discussions can help stimulate ideas as members of a group share experiences through a process called "guided discovery".
- Discussions are most effective when a trained (experienced) leader controls the overall process in an organized manner.
- Discussions are appropriate if only a few major (simple) topics are being covered, and when it is acceptable to have several outcomes (i.e. it is not necessary to reach consensus or derive a single conclusion).

ADVANTAGES:

- Discussions allow multiple views and opinions to be expressed.
- Discussions provide an informal atmosphere, and allow everyone to express and listen to opinions that are presented with equal weight.
- Two way communication and each is made to participate.
- Each trainee is benefited.

DRAWBACKS:

- Discussions can get bogged-down or begin to taper-off if the leader is not experienced in controlling the group.
- Discussions can be dominated by a strong member of the group,

unless the leader controls the overall process to insure everyone is given equal time and the same level of respect.

- Formal discussions require a well-defined purpose or objective, a reasonable time limit, and a well-trained leader. It is not just a bunch of people sitting around a table gabbing with each other.

### *What is a Case Study?*

- When the opposing viewpoints of a realistic situation (or event) are presented to a group, and a logical analysis involving a "judgment call" must be conducted to arrive at a conclusion, this is called a case study.
- A case study can be presented orally or as a written document, but the process of analyzing and evaluating opposing viewpoints to reach a reasonable conclusion is the same.

### *When Should A Case Study be Used?*

- A case study is a useful method when there is no clear-cut or easy solution to a problem.
- Case studies are useful when real-life situations can be used as examples to highlight the training topic(s) being covered.
- In situations when multiple viewpoints must be considered, case studies can help participants evaluate the merits of different arguments.

ADVANTAGES:

- A well chosen case study will be relevant to all participants.
- Everyone is actively engaged in the case study process.
- Individuals are forced to make a decision, and then defend it.

DRAWBACKS:

- The case study must be relevant, realistic, and appropriate.
- The case study scenario must be carefully worded to avoid bias, or imply that one position is stronger than the other.

- Although the final outcome of a case study analysis forces each individual to draw a conclusion and make a decision, it should be recognized that it is not necessary to reach consensus (i.e. it is not a mock trial), and participants should be reminded it is a training exercise.

## *What is Role Playing?*

- When participants and/or trainers act out parts in an open-ended story intended to highlight conflicting viewpoints, this is called role playing.
- Role playing is different from stage drama because the lines (scripts) are not pre-determined, the players originate their dialogue in real time, and as the scenario unfolds they interact to develop an outcome.
- Role-playing, or "learning through acting", is a technique that requires participants to perform a task in a realistic situation simulating "real life". This type of exercise is an effective means to take in and absorb the content and substance of new ideas.
- It facilitates an active understanding of the information and gives participants the opportunity to apply new skills and abilities.
- The participants not only rehearse their own behavior in a particular situation, but also have the opportunity as a group to evaluate how effective the staged resolution of the problem actually was.

## *When Should Role Playing be Used?*

- Role playing is effective when the topic involves person-to-person communication and/or interaction.
- Role playing can allow everyone to participate.
- The overall mood a training session can be improved by the excitement that role playing provides.

ADVANTAGES:

- Role playing is an excellent forum for exploring the topics of ethics and conflict resolution.

- Participants can "feel a new viewpoint" through dynamic role playing.
- Individuals are often inclined to express true feelings when role playing.
- The group listens better and learns more because they are seeing and hearing the subject matter as it is acted out.

DRAWBACKS:

- Role playing requires careful selection of situations to be effective.
- Role playing impedes free expression if participants are not volunteers.
- The themes for role playing exercises must avoid potential conflicts with the principles of the Scout Oath/Law, religious teaching, or other groups.

### *What is A Senstivity?*

- This method is the youngest of methods. It belongs to the "T" group, a highly participative learning method whose purpose is to improve trainee's skills in working with other people by increasing the ability to appreciate how others are reacting to one's own behavior.
- It aims at making the trainees more sensitive to their environment and customer's behavior.
- It involves role-playing and interacting with other member trainees so as to increase the self-ability to listen and understand the customer.

### *When Should Senstivity be Used?*

- Sensitivity is to find out the rationale behind others' behavior and suggest the ways to adjust.

ADVANTAGES:

- Sensitivity is participative type imparting knowledge and improving skills.

- Makes sensitive to environment and customer behavior.
- It is role playing and analysis.
- Building of self-confidence.

DRAWBACKS:

- Selectivity is not possible for all to be sensitive.
- It is costlier.
- It is time consuming.
- Participants take it lightly.

## SALES FORCE ORIENTATION

Once the sales people are selected and trained, they are to be inducted or oriented and placed on the jobs.

### *What it Means?*

Orientation is also called as induction. Induction process is designed to provide a new salesperson with the informal he or she needs to function comfortably and effectively in the organization he or she joins.

Typically orientation or induction conveys three types of information namely, general information about the daily work routine, a review of the organizational history, and a detailed presentation - in the form of hand book or manual of organization's policies , work rules and employee benefits.

PURPOSE OF INDUCTION

- To make sales people to feel at home.
- To make them know the ground realities.
- To expose to all the areas of the organization.
- To create an impression that lasts longer.

ORIENTATION PROGRAM:

Formal induction program is quite elaborate and is spread over a couple of weeks or months. Most formal programs consist of three stages:

- A general introduction to the organization, often given by human reserve department.
- Specific orientation to the department and the job.
- Follow-up meeting to verify that the significant issues have been addressed and employee questions have been answered.

### *Tenets of An Effective Orientation Program*

- Foster an understanding of the campus culture, its values, and its diversity
- Help the new employee make a successful adjustment to the new job
- Help the new employee understand her role and how she fits into the total organization
- Help the new employee achieve objectives and shorten the learning curve
- Help the new employee develop a positive working relationship by building a foundation of knowledge about campus mission, objectives, policies, organization structure, and functions

### *Sales Force Placement:*

Sales placement is taken as the allocation of sales people to jobs. It is the assignment or reassignment to an employee of a new or different job. Placement includes initial assignment of a new employees and promotion, transfer or demotion of present employees. Here we are concerned with new employees.

The process of placement can be configured in the form as:

- Collect the data about the employee.
- Conduct his or her profile.
- Which sub-group profile does the individuals profile best fits
- Compare sub-group profile to job framing profiles.
- Which job family profile does sub-group profile best fit.
- Assign the individual to the job family.
- Assign the individual to specific job after further counseling and assessment.

To sum up, the employees are placed on their jobs. In case of sales people they are assigned to sales territories and given the targets for achievement in the form of sales quotas.

## SUMMARY

### *Sales Training*

Sales training is an important part of a sales manager's responsibility. Having the proper training in place helps ensure the success of your sales goals When putting together your sales training program, consider how it interacts with your marketing, technical, customer, and product considerations. Make sure you tailor, integrate, deliver, and measure your training appropriately. Be sure to read the other articles on this site for more information on how to improve your sales effectiveness.

### *Sales Orientation*

Changing an organisational culture is not an easy process to undertake, but if done correctly can lead to long and lasting success. When you plans are carefully made and built upon the proper foundation, implementing change can be much easier, and the chances of success are much improved. The previous eight steps all play a part in achieving this change and making change and improvement a part of company culture. Only when this is fully engrained can true victory be declared.

### *Sales Placement*

It is a task of assigning or allocating the newly prepared employees to job for which they are selected. In real sense it is assignment or reassignment of an employee to job may be new or different jobs.

## REFRENCES


- ASM book by C.N.Sontakki
- http://www.businessballs.com/salestraining.htm
- www.actionselling.com/sales-training/sales-training-programs?
- www.businessdictionary.com/definition/sales-orientation.html?

# SALES FORCE COMPENSATION

## BASICS ABOUT SALES FORCE

Salespeople are a company's ambassadors to the world. They actively promote the company and its products and services. They are the front line between the company and its customers, and are typically the driving force of revenues - top-line company growth. These employees have a direct impact on how the marketplace perceives their employer and its products.

The way salespeople conduct themselves is often a reflection of the company's sales compensation program; and how well the company does is often a reflection of the effectiveness of its commission program. A well designed sales compensation program focuses salespeople on activities that support the company's business objectives, and, in turn, rewards those salespeople for their contributions.

Base salary, commissions, and sales prizes make up the bulk of a typical salesperson's compensation package, but the specifics vary by industry. Stock options grants to salespeople are becoming more widespread too.

In a snapshot Sales compensation packages typically comprise one or more of the following components:

- Base Salary
- Periodic incentives tied to short-term goals
- Annual Incentives tied to longer-term sales activities

- Commission-based incentives
- Perquisites to facilitate sales efforts
- Stock options

## BASE SALARIES

Paying a base salary that assures salespeople a steady income is a good idea. A guaranteed salary provides salespeople the comfort of knowing that despite good and bad economies, streaks and slumps, they can maintain their current lifestyle.

A salesperson's commission is typically based on either a percentage of sold revenues or profit margins. Commissions usually account for 30 to 50 percent of a salesperson's cash compensation package, which means that commissions routinely run between 43 and 100 percent of base pay. The percentage that commissions contribute to a salesperson's compensation depends on factors such as required technical knowledge, sales cycle time, product profitability, and whether the sale is dependent on the skill of the salesperson.

Commissions will account for a larger portion of pay when the sales cycle is short, the sales highly profitable, and sales dependent on the skills of the sales person. Commissions play a smaller role when the sale requires greater technical knowledge and when the sales cycle is long.

This is not to say that total compensation is necessarily lower for salespeople with greater technical knowledge or those selling products with slower sales cycles, rather, the mix of pay is weighted more toward base pay and less toward commissions so that the total cash pay earned is reasonable. Companies don't want to penalize salespeople for selling products with less commission potential if those products are an important part of the corporate strategy. Similarly, if a salesperson is responsible for a product that's an easy sell, the company wants to make sure there is the maximum incentive to sell as much as possible - therefore, less emphasis on base pay and more emphasis on commissions.

Commissions can vary within a commission plan, reflecting the priorities of the company. If the company wants to build market share, it may pay larger commissions for selling products to new clients. Commissions are also higher when new products are introduced, especially if they are more profitable. Clearly, commission plans are constructed with great care. A poorly designed plan can have unintended results such as rewarding employees for the sale of new products that cannibalize more profitable ones.

Most commission plans place no limits on what a salesperson can earn. In some instances, if a certain sales threshold has been met, the commission percentage can increase. Regardless, commissions are one of the simplest and most direct forms of pay-for-performance. Underlying the commission plan is one of the appeals of a sales position: unlimited income potential.

## CREATING AN IDEAL COMPENSATION PROGRAM

Sales compensation is a crucial factor in motivation. It is the sales executive's best strategic tool to drive sales performance and motivate specific selling behaviours. When designing sales compensation plans, one of the most important steps is to identify the appropriate measures on which your sales representatives will be paid. A combination of salary, commission and bonus is usually most effective. The question then becomes how to successfully blend all three that will entice achievers, as well as reward them according to performance. Nevertheless, the plan needs to be kept as simple as possible.

**The total compensation mix: what does it entail?**

Total compensation depends on the complexity of the sales person's selling tasks. The mix between performance and fixed pay depends on:

1) Balancing salesperson and company needs;
2) The type of salesperson you want to attract;
3) The salesperson's influence on the sale;
4) The type of product or service sold; and

5) Rewarding the salesperson's specific actions or results most important to the company's success.

Sales force compensation involves not merely salary, commission and bonus but also fringe benefits and reimbursed expenses - though these last two are considered non-compensatory since they are not influenced by sales results.

**An ideal compensation plan should:**

- reward positive action and superior results important to the success of your company;
- the mix between fixed and performance pay should reflect the type salesperson you wish to attract and the salesperson's influence on the sales;
- the total level of compensation ought to reflect the complexity of the sale.

## *Types of Sales Force Compensation*

DIRECT COMPENSATION consists of:

- Fixed pay (salary)
- Performance pay (commission)
- Deferred performance pay (bonus)
- Fringe benefits (Social security/insurance, group insurance, optional profit sharing etc.)
- Reimbursed expenses

## *Constructing a total compensation plan*

In constructing a compensation program, you first decide on the total dollars of compensation for a top salesperson in your industry - the "target" compensation. Your next decision is dividing those dollars between fixed and performance pay. The total compensation appropriate for a successful salesperson is determined by the complexity of the sale and type of selling. You define a "successful salesperson" as someone who ranks in the top 25 percent of your sales force in terms of results (based on annual dollars of sales or margin and growth). The following are simply a guideline.

- A successful/top salesperson involved in a long, complex, multistep, consultative, partnership sales process should receive over US$100,000 (or your currency equivalent) annually in compensation regardless of the mix between fixed and performance pay.
- A salesperson involved in multi-level relationship sales, which includes the re-purchase of existing systems, which may require some post-sale service, generally receives US$60,000 to US$100,000 (or your currency equivalent) annually in total direct compensation regardless of the mix between fixed and performance pay. These people use more transactional sales to hunt or harvest and have titles such as "Territory Representative" or "Account Manager".
- A successful salesperson involved in route sales of homogeneous products or services, requiring a multitude of daily customer visits and feature selling and order taking from a person delegated by the buyer's decision maker generally receives under US$60,000 in total direct compensation, regardless of the mix between fixed and performance pay.
- Salespeople selling and servicing grocery stores with food products, drugstores and giftware, midsized businesses with temporary help services and manufacturers with die casting or injecting molding products generally receive annual direct compensation of under US$60,000 (or your currency equivalent).

Experience shows that more fixed dollars of compensation paid allows the management to more easily direct/control a salesperson.

### *Surveys Exposed*

According to Equation research, their 3,000 respondent, 2005 sales compensation survey results indicated the following:

- Top sales people averaged with a total compensation of $157,234, mid-level performers with an average of $94,872 and for low performers with $64,844.

- Fifty to 60% of the total compensation was fixed pay for all three of the above groups.

In a 2009 Watson Wyatt survey on sales force compensation and management reveals that sales and HR executives (129 respondents), at large cross-section of North American industries, are confident in the current alignment between sales performance and sales compensation. Seventy-nine percent report their top performers earn the highest levels of sales compensation, indicating a strong link between pay and performance.

### *Correct Mix of Performance and Fixed Pay*

The mix between performance and fixed pay depends on:

1- Balancing the company's and salespeople's needs - [The company needs to attract, retain and motivate salespeople who produce a desired level of sales at a cost that generates profits and allows necessary percentage returns on sales and invested capital. It must reflect the company's culture, strategy and position on the growth curve.];

2- The type of salesperson you want to attract - [Fixed pay oriented compensation plans generally attract salespeople who are team players, ambitious to climb the executive ladder, steady rather than top performers, farmers rather than hunters and more comfortable selling presold products. On the other hand, Performance pay type compensation plans generally attract aggressive career salespeople, hunters rather than farmers and those with little ambition for promotion into management.];

3- The salesperson's influence on the sale - [Ex: A company with all performance pay means the salesperson has a great deal or total influence on the sale.];

4- The type of product or service sold - [An order taker type of salesperson rather than an active seller, whereby he/she has less influence on the sale];

5- Rewarding the salesperson's specific actions or results most important to the company's success - [The sales force compensation plan must reward actions and results on the part of salespeople that are most important to the company's success. Generally, a commission is used to reward results and a bonus is used to reward activities or exceeding goals. A group bonus might also be considered to reward teamwork.]

If sales people have a pricing window and/or discretion to give discounts, allowances and promotions, a portion of their compensation should be based on dollars of gross margin rather than revenue for their territory. For example, a women's apparel manufacturer pays a commission rate on gross margin dollars because salespeople have some discretion to negotiate price.

To prevent making your compensation plan too complicated, limit the performance pay metrics to three actions or results - all of which are controllable by the individual.

It is suggested that each year, the company's sales leadership should re-evaluate the sales force compensation program as business constantly evolves.

### *New Product Placement*

Many firms reward new product placement through their compensation plans. A salesperson exerts the most influence on a customer's decision during a product or service's introduction and the least during a product or service's decline. As such, some firms pay a higher level and rate of performance pay on new products and a lesser level and rate of performance pay on mature or declining products or markets.

### *Transactional Versus Consultative Selling*

Salespeople involved in transactional sales will receive rewards in fewer performance areas than those involved in the more complex consultative sales. Salespeople involved in farming or maintenance will receive less variable pay than those involved in hunting or new account acquisition.

### *Support Personnel*

If your firm supports direct salespeople with product specialists, sales engineers or customer service representatives, consider performance pay for these people as it will encourage them to be team players for the good of the organization.

## CHANNEL PARTNERS (OUTSIDE/ INDEPENDENT REPRESENTATIVE ORGANIZATIONS)

Brokers, distributors and outside sales representative organizations generally receive 100 percent performance pay from the firms whose products they sell. However, channel partners need specific rewards for positive action and results important to the success of your company. For your indirect sales force to become partners rather than adversaries, they require training and correct monetary incentives. Apply the same criteria for your indirect sales force that you did for your direct people. Generally, your channel partners compensate their salespeople with a plan similar to the one you use to compensate the channel partners.

### *Change Management and Implementation*

One way to sell compensation changes to the sales force involves including them in the decision-making process. Select a representative group to participate in the analysis, suggest changes and anticipate problems. Address concerns by showing how the new compensation plan can increase annual pay. Annual performance changes must be announced before the year begins so that salespeople have time to adjust their thinking activities.

### *When it's all said and done*

Sales compensation is a tricky business as there are a number of payment models to choose from and each method has its pros and cons. Commissions motivate employees to sell harder, while salaries create loyal employees. To attract, motivate and retain the best salespeople, you pay them what they are worth. Performance pay that rewards positive action along with results can create windfall earnings for salespeople and increased revenues for the company. However, in the end, it is the sales manager's job to make the salespeople successful so they can fully monetize on the reward plan.

### *Review of the Sales Force Compensation Program*

A review of the sales plan is needed to confirm that the rewards sales employees receive are commensurate for their efforts and skill sets utilized to achieve their sales goals. The Internet has opened new markets and new methods for marketing and selling products. A sales plan designed to pay a sales employee for calling on customers and presenting the product or services in a traditional manner does not pay appropriately for a sales employee who is able to generate sales using the Internet. Companies could find themselves overpaying sales employees if the earnings formulas are based on personal selling while the employee is able to sell significantly more using new technologies. One could argue that more sales result in more profit for the company, but most plans accelerate the earnings rate once the sales target has been achieved. If the target or quota does not reflect differences in selling strategies, sales employees who are able to utilize new technologies will prosper and other sales employees will become de-motivated and possibly leave the organization.

The competitive marketplace is constantly changing. Products once sold by specialty retailers are now appearing in discount stores. The sales employee selling to large discount chains has a different selling job than the sales employee selling to specialty stores. Sales plans should be designed to reflect this difference.

Today, businesses find themselves constantly revising their business plans to be successful in this fast changing environment. The "most important" product this week may not be the same "most important" product from last week. Sales employees tend to sell the products they know best even if they do not exactly align with the company's objectives. A ten-year-old sales plan may not be flexible enough to provide focus for sales employees in these times of product emphasis change.

There may be sections in sales plans which are "bombs" waiting to explode. A few years ago the sales plans for cellular telephone salespeople in Southern Florida provided commission earnings based on units sold. There were step levels where the commission rate increased as sales volume increased above target or quota. Along came Hurricane Andrew and cell phone sales skyrocketed. There was no other means of communication; people had to purchase cell phones to handle daily activities and to communicate. Sales incentive payments also skyrocketed but through no increased effort on the part of the sales employee. That plan was later changed to exclude an amount of sales generated by actions beyond the sales employee's control.

We've found that the director of sales or the president designed most sales compensation plans in smaller companies. The plans were biased toward the designer's interests. Plans often had unrealistic quotas, payment schedules and product goals that focus the sales employee on the designer's interests, not necessarily the interests of the organization.

A sales compensation plan is not a "one size fits all" proposition. The organization needs to review the goals for the organization, each product line, each sales employee's abilities, and desired profit contribution for each product line. Sales compensation plans should align the employee's goals and rewards with the achievement of the organizations goals and strategic objectives.

Companies tend to think of summer as a time for reflection and vacation, but this is the time to review the sales compensation plans. By beginning now, companies can review the plans, model possible changes, cost out changes, design new plan components, and prepare communications programs so that revisions will be ready for introduction before the New Year begins. Waiting until November to begin a sales compensation plan review usually results in a quickly formulated, untested, poorly communicated plan, which is not accepted readily or favourably by the sales force.

## SOURCE

1. http://salesforcecompensation.blogspot.in/

2. http://www.bizcompare.com/blog/sales-compensation/sales-force-dynamics-instituting-an-ideal-compensation-plan/
3. http://savvychicksmedia.com/topic/marketing/sales-force-dynamics-instituting-ideal-compensation-plan/

# SALES FORCE CONTROL / PERFORMANCE APPRAISAL OF SALES FORCE

## INTRODUCTION

Sales Force Control, performance appraisal (PA), performance review, performance evaluation, (career) development discussion, or employee appraisal is a method by which the job performance of an employee is evaluated. Performance appraisals are a part of career development and consist of regular reviews of employee performance within organizations. A performance appraisal is a systematic and periodic process that assesses an individual employee's job performance and productivity in relation to certain pre-established criteria and organizational objectives. Other aspects of individual employees are considered as well, such as organizational citizenship behavior, accomplishments, potential for future improvement, strengths and weaknesses, etc. To collect PA data, there are three main methods: objective production, personnel, and judgmental evaluation. Some applications of PA are compensation, performance improvement, promotions, termination, test validation, and more. While there are many potential benefits of PA, there are also some potential drawbacks. For example, PA can help facilitate management-employee communication; however, PA may result in legal issues if not executed appropriately as many employees tend to be unsatisfied with the PA process. PAs created in and determined as useful in the India are not necessarily able to be transferable cross-culturally. There are a number of potential benefits of organizational performance management conducting formal performance appraisals (PAs). There has been a general consensus in the belief that PAs lead to positive implications of organizations. Furthermore, PAs can benefit an organization's effectiveness. One way is PAs can often lead to giving individual workers feedback about their job performance.

## MEANING OF SALES FORCE CONTROL

Managing and motivating a sales team is essential to the success of any business. Sales professionals are the fuel that drives an organization. When that team is staffed with talented people working as a cohesive unit, sales are made and prospects turn into customers. When the team is not working at maximum efficiency, the company cannot grow and thrive. There are several tactics a sales manager can employ to improve productivity. Businesses can decide between two types of sales teams or use a combination of both. Outside sales representatives, also called field reps, work independently to generate sales. This type of sales force structure works best with responsible, self-starters who need little supervision. They travel to customer locations to pitch products that require demonstration. Inside sales representatives, also called telemarketers, spend most of their time on the telephone talking with prospective customers or making appointments for customers to come to them. The benefits of hiring a competent sales team include increased brand awareness, heightened company loyalty, and increased revenues. It may take some trial and error during the hiring process, but finding effective salespeople takes patience. Once established, a sales force creates excitement around the products and services they sell. Using social media is another way to connect with potential customers, promote sales campaigns, and provide information. The process of sales force control mainly includes the following four stages:

- Establishing sales performance standards
- Measuring actual performance
- Comparing actual performance against the standards

- Taking necessary actions

Controlling is determining what is being accomplished i.e. evaluating the performances and if necessary applying corrective measures so that performance takes place according to plans. Basically, sales control is to identify the weaknesses in the sales efforts, to determine their causes and to correct them rapidly with the sole objective of obtaining maximum profit. Sales force control enables the management to know whether the salesmen are performing to the best of their abilities.

The Main objective of SALES FORCE CONTROL is to maximize sales and to ensure optimum usage of selling expense so as to maximize the profit for the organization.

## IMPORTANCE/ NEED & SIGNIFICANCE

A sales force, whether it consists of one person or 100 people, largely determines a company's success or failure. When developing a sales force, hiring managers must have the resources necessary to attract the optimal people for the team as well as have a clear idea of what their profiles, or resumes, may look like. Armed with these resources and knowledge, managers can build a team that benefits the company in every aspect. The ultimate function of a sales force is to generate revenue for the company through the sale of its products or services. But the role of a properly developed and trained sales team encompasses so much more. They must build customer satisfaction and trust throughout the sales cycle. This creates repeat business and new business from customer referrals. Many companies have added a customer satisfaction metric to sales team evaluations. In the past these evaluations focused mostly on sales data. Truly professional sales people also strive to represent their company in the best possible light, even in their personal lives. In addition to generating income, the sales force builds trust with customers. Sales representatives engage customers at all stages of the relationship. New customers need interaction and opportunities to learn about the brand. Current customers gain trust through consistent follow-up and communication with the sales representative. Sales representatives also work to re-engage previous customers through promotions, discounts, and communications. Building trust throughout the customer sales cycle increases customer satisfaction.

The following points describe the importance, need and significance of SALES FORCE CONTROL:

- It identifies the drawbacks and weaknesses of the sales force which can be then removed to increase their productivity.

A company can identify its weaknesses and drawbacks with the help of SALES FORCE CONTROL. Therefore the company can analyze its shortcomings and rectify/remove the shortcomings in order to maximize the productivity of sales force.

- It increases the sales, profits and thereby results in optimum usage of the sales force.

With the help of SALES FORCE CONTROL the company can increase the efficiency of its sales force thereby increasing the sales resulting in an increase in the company's profits.

- It helps in the evaluation of a salesman's worth i.e. whether the sales force is paid in accordance with their ability, skills and performance.

With the help of SALES FORCE CONTROL a company can draw out the pay scale of the sales force. It can motivate those sales personnel who were under paid because there will be an increase in their pay scale. Also company can decrease its expenses by curtailing the salary paid to overpaid employees.

- It helps in the identification of the company's most profitable products, the territories from which they are getting the maximum business.

With the help of SALES FORCE CONTROL a company can analyze the products and the areas from which it draws the maximum profits. The company can spend more on marketing in those areas and for those products. Also the underperforming products/territories can either be revamped or discontinued which will again decrease the company's expenses.

- It also helps to draw the compensation plan of the sales force effectively.

With the help of sales force control the company can draw out the perfect compensation plan (bonuses, overtime, medical assistance etc.) for its sales force. This will motivate the sales force to perform to the best of their abilities and skill.

## STEPS IN SALES FORCE CONTROL / SALES CONTROL PROCESS

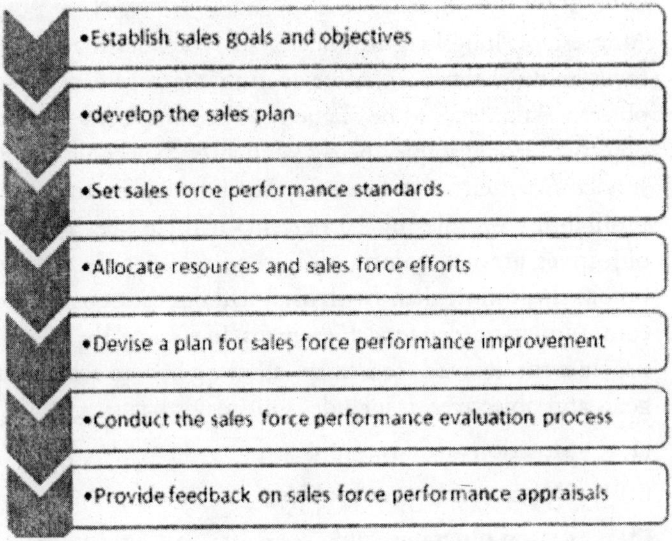


Outcome-based measures can be separated into sales efforts, sales results, and profitability indices. Sales efforts include such measures as number of sales calls made, selling expenses as a percentage of sales volume, and number of service calls. Sales results include measures such as number of orders obtained, dollar sales volume, number of new accounts, and collections of accounts receivable. Profitability indices include net profit contribution, and performance as measured by financial/economic indicators, such as return on investment, return on sales, return on assets, and return on assets managed. Behavior-based outcomes include sales-related activities such as customer relations, territory management, report preparation and timely submission, product knowledge, and personal characteristics. Successful sales organizations usually employ a mixture of quantitative and qualitative performance standards. Competence assessment, which tries to determine the characteristics needed to do a job rather than the specific tasks of the job, has been successfully used to select high-achieving salespeople. Professional development measures for assessing sales force performance include professional selling skills, professional knowledge, and personal characteristics.

1. Establish different types of sales goals and objectives, and develop the sales plan

   After establishing long-run sales goals, the sales manager can focus on the shorter-run, more quantifiable targets, called sales objectives that should be aligned to the company's goals and objectives. For example, these goals may be to become the most service-oriented sales force in the industry or to increase profitability on sales by 10 percent. If these sales goals and objectives are not communicated to salespeople, they can become little more than "wish lists" without the organizational commitment needed for achievement. In essence, the sales plan provides the detailed "road map" showing how to achieve sales goals and objectives. It includes four major parts:

   (1) Situation analysis,

   (2) Opportunities and problems,

   (3) Action programs, and

   (4) Performance evaluation systems.

2. Setting sales performance standards:

   Performance standards are planned achievement levels the sales organization expects to reach at progressive intervals throughout the year. Ideally, they should be agreements between subordinates and superiors as to what level of performance is to be acceptable in some future period, and they should be formalized based on the detailed job description for the sales subordinate. In setting performance standards for the sales force, managers need to consider efforts expended as well as results obtained. Business-to-business sales may require several months of intense sales efforts before the prospective buyer makes a final decision. Thus, where there's a time lag between effort and tangible results, sales managers must use qualitative, as well as quantitative, measures in setting sales performance standards.

3. Allocate resources and efforts through sales quotas.

   There are four types of sales quotas: sales volume, financial, activity, and combination. The rationale to use a specific type of sales quota is largely based on the quantitative and qualitative sales goals a salesperson is expected to achieve in a given time frame. Three variants of volumes quotas are dollar-based sales quotas, unit volume quotas, and point quotas. Two categories of financial quotas are expense quotas and profit quotas. Activity quotas are measured by factors such as the number of prospects called on, number of demonstrations made, number of displays set up, and number of new accounts established. Combination quotas are used when management wants to control the performance of both the selling and non-selling activities of the sales force. These quotas generally use points as a common measuring tool to overcome the difficulty of evaluating the different units used across quotas.

4. Measuring actual performance

   An effective performance evaluation monitoring system (PEMS) has three stages: performance planning, performance appraisal, and performance review. Specific steps in the performance measurement and evaluation process include (a) establish sales goals and objectives, (b) develop the sales plan, (c) set performance standards, (d) allocate resources and sales force efforts in implementing the sales plan, and (e) evaluate sales force performance and implement corrective actions, if needed.

5. Provide feedback and evaluation, and improve sales force performance.

   Four widely used evaluation techniques are descriptive statements, graphic rating scales, behaviorally anchored rating scales (BARS), and management by objectives (MBO). Descriptive statements about a salesperson may be short responses to a series of specific criteria such as job knowledge, territorial management, customer relations, personal qualities, or sales results. Two commonly employed devices in graphic rating scales are "semantic differential" and Likert-type scales. The semantic differential uses bipolar adjective extremes to anchor several scale segments. Likert-type scales provide descriptive anchors under each segment of the scale. BARS, which concentrate on measuring behaviors key to performance that the individual salesperson can control, includes four basic steps: (a) identify critical incidents, (b) refine critical incidents into performance dimensions, (c) rate the effectiveness of the described behaviors, and (d) select a set of incidents as behavioral anchors for the performance dimension. MBO involves mutual goal setting by the sales manager and the sales representative, who jointly agree on the salesperson's specific goals or performance targets for the coming period. Traditional performance evaluation systems have limitations including the halo effect, central tendency, varying evaluation standards, psychological resistance to negative evaluations, recent performance bias, no outcome focus, inadequate sampling of job activities, political concerns, fear of reprisal, interpersonal bias, questionable personality traits, and the influence of special organizational use. Prompt evaluation feedback should be provided to salespeople, so they can take measures to enhance their performance by improving selling skills and ultimately their sales performance through sales training programs.

6. Apply twenty-first century sales force performance appraisal methods.

   Current developments in the area of sales force performance appraisals include 360-degree performance perspectives, performance appraisals of team selling, and performance review ranking systems. Just as in evaluating individual sales force members, team performance evaluation involves selecting the relevant performance criteria and employing appropriate appraisal methods. The 360-degree performance appraisal process systematically elicits information on a salesperson's skills, abilities, and behaviors from various individuals with whom the salesperson is in ongoing contact all internal and external constituents, including the sales manager, sales team peers, sales subordinates, other departmental coworkers, purchasing managers, and accounts payable managers. Also included is a self-assessment, thus providing appraisal from many different perspectives. Performance review ranking entails sales managers evaluating each of their salespeople by ranking them using multiple performance dimensions and then placing them in different performance categories using a scale (e.g., A _ excellent performance, B _ above-average performance, C _ average performance, D _ satisfactory performance, and E _ sub-par performance).

## SALES FORCE CONTROL TECHNIQUES / METHODS FOR PERFORMANCE APPRAISAL OF SALESMAN

### *Qualitative Methods*

1. Evaluation by Sales Supervisors:

   Sales supervisors review the salesmen's working and give report regarding their punctuality, cooperation, reliability, Salesmanship, personality, adaptability, initiative etc. Sales supervisors can review working of salesmen through personal contact, correspondence and through salesmen's reports. In personal contacts, sales supervisors personally check the working of salesmen. E.g. they supervise their method of making sates call, their routing and travelling plan, their selling expenses etc. in control through correspondence, necessary instructions are passed to the salesmen through correspondence and compliance of instructions is also received through correspondence. In control through salesmen's reports, salesmen are supposed to give detailed report of their activities in the prescribed format. These reports can be on daily, weekly, monthly, quarterly basis. Thus, sales supervisors evaluate the performance of salesmen through correspondence or through personal contact.

**Evaluation on the Basis of Information Given by Customers:** Top sales executives make contacts with regular customers and get feedback about salesmen regarding product knowledge, awareness of customer's needs, relationship with customers, attending customers' complaints, salesmen's behavior etc. This feedback helps sales executives to form opinion regarding sales personnel.

**Evaluation on the Basis of Information Given by Other Groups:** Other groups here refer to dealers, distribution, wholesalers, retailers, etc. The persons also interact with salesmen. Sales executives contact such groups to get feedback about the working of sales personnel.

**Routing and Scheduling:** Routing here refers to sales personnel movement plan in their sales territory. Scheduling refers to date and time of making sales call. Well-thought out routing and scheduling plan helps to control travelling expenses, selling expenses, boarding ,lodging expenses of salesmen and increase call frequency of sales force. By preparing routing and scheduling plan in advance, sales managers can know the date, time and place where salesmen are working/making sales call. In other words, salesmen become conscious of their working and movements. If they do not make sales calls as per as their schedule plan, they may he caught and punished.

**Sales Audit:** Sales audit is a systematic and unbiased review and appraisal of different selling functions performed by different sales personnel. Sales audit compares the actual performance with the pre-determined standards. It identi?es strengths and weaknesses of sales department. It evaluates the overall selling strategy, policy, procedures, authority and responsibility given to each individual. It helps to measure the effectiveness of sales organization as a whole.

### *Quantitative Methods*

1. Comparison of Salesmen's Performance with Sales Quota:

   Sales quota is a quantitative measure of sales defined in terms of units or rupees. Sales quotas are decided keeping in view the sales potential of territory, last year's sales, proposed changes in promotion mix, marketing-mix, level of competition etc. Actual sales achieved by salesmen are compared with sales quota. If actual sales are less than quota. It indicates negative performance.

2. Selling Expense Ratio:

   For controlling selling expenses, ratio of selling expenses with sales is computed in each territory. This ratio is compared with standards fixed by top executives. The ratio of different territory/ products can also be compared with each other and with the ratios of previous periods. Low selling expenses ratio is a positive indicator as it implies optimum utilization of selling expenses.

3. Number of Sales Calls per Day:

It means average number of consumers contacted by salesman in a day. Sales calls per day of different salesmen are compared with each other who are selling similar products in similar market situation. Higher sales calls per day are a positive indicator of performance of sales force.

4. Order-Call Ratio:

   It means ratio of orders procured with total number of sales calls made by salesmen. Higher ratio is better as it indicates better salesmanship qualities and better convincing abilities.

5. Percentage of Market Share:

   Sales executives set target market percentages for each territory i.e: , the proportion of total market to be covered by salesmen in each sales territory. These percentages are compared with actual percentages of market share. It helps to measure the effectiveness of salesmen working in that territory. If actual percentage of market share is more than target percentage share, then it indicates efficiency of salesmen.

6. Average order size:

   Average order size of different sales personnel is compared with each other. Higher order size indicates efficiency of sales Personnel.

7. Contribution to profits:

Contribution to profits is an indicator of salesmen's performance. The salesman who contributes more to pro?ts is treated as more efficient. The company computes contribution of each salesman in the total pro?t of the organization by multiplying sales achieved by salesman with gross pro?t ratio or net profit ratio.

8. Report of Field Sales Executives:

Sales executives use ?eld-sales reports to determine whether sales personnel are making proper number of calls. These reports also provide information about miles travelled by salesmen, sales made, number of customer complaints attended, etc. Field sales executives prepare sales personnel evaluation reports which are abo known as Progress Reports. These reports help sales executives to evaluate performance of sales personnel.

9. Ratio of Actual Sales with Sales Potential:

Sales potential of different market areas is different. So, mere comparing actual sales of different market areas with each other are not sufficient. There is also need for comparing actual sales with its sales potential in the market areas. For this, ratio of actual sales to sales potential is computed. Higher ratio indicates better market coverage.

10. Comparison of Current Year's Sales with Past Year's Sales:

Control over sales personnel can also be exercised by comparing current year's sales with past year's sates. If current year's sales are rising in comparison to last year's sales, then it indicates favorable performance of sales personnel. But if current year's Sales are less than past year's sales, then it indicates poor performance of sales force and it is an alarming sign for the business unit.

No single method of controlling sales personnel is complete in itself. Sales manager should use both quantitative and qualitative methods for controlling and evaluating sales personnel. Results based on single method can be wrong. So combination of methods should be used for controlling sales personnel.

## ESSENTIALS OF GOOD SALES FORCE CONTROL SYSTEM

Every good sales control system has distinguished characteristics. Some of them are discussed below:

**SETTING OF STANDARDS:** Various standards need to be set in relation to expenses, volume, number of sales calls, number of hours etc. This standard should be maintained while keeping in mind the individual characters. Every sales guy is different from the other so standards need to be maintained accordingly.

**WELL DEFINED OBJECTIVES:** Objective needs to be well defined. If we want to increase sales it should be clearly stated. For example, if sales are to be increased from 20,000 to 30,000 in 1 year then that should be stated clearly. There must be no confusion whatsoever.

**SIMPLICITY:** Control system should be simple. It must not be difficult to understand for managers as well as field executives. The salespersons should be clearly educated about the system. Standards mentioned should be clear to them. It must be easy to understand. If the standards are not clear they might backfire and lead to loss of motivation.

**IMPARTIAL:** The sales control standard set should be impartial. There must not be multiple standards for different persons. If there is a partial system then the other salesmen will feel unsatisfied and will lead to decrease in performance of the individual.

**FLEXIBLE:** Sales control should be flexible. It should be able to adjust to various different environments both internal and external. It should be made flexible in such a way that it is able to revise its standards if needed.

**ECONOMICAL:** Sales control system should be economical. Benefits of control system should be more than cost of control system. It should be exercised on crucial points only and should be avoided elsewhere to reduce unnecessary cost.

**MOTIVATIONAL:** Control system has to be motivational in nature. The achievers should be awarded. It will then motivate the under-achievers to perform better. This will lead to improved efficiency of the organization as a whole.

CONTINUITY: A control system should be continuous in nature so that that mistakes are corrected at the earliest and chances of their recurrence are minimal.

FUTURE-ORIENTED: The sales force control system should be future oriented so that it is able to provide remedial measures if performances are not up to the standards. It will lead to improve in performance score.

SUITABILITY: The sales force control system should be suitable to the organization for which it is designed. Big enterprises and small enterprises have different sales force control systems. Same standards are not applicable to all the organization. Control system most suited to the organization are needs to be selected.

*Control of Critical Points:*

The critical points should be prioritized. They should be mentioned from the very beginning and serve as a very important part in ensuring organizational success. It states that managers should not be too focused on less important things. Rather they should focus on the critical points and ensure success.

## LIMITATIONS OF SALES FORCE CONTROL SYSTEM

Following are the limitations and difficulties of sales force control system:

HUMAN PROBLEMS: Salesmen cannot work like machines. They are like us all humans. Sales force control system sometimes ignores the human element. Salesmen often feel that control system is set up just to find their shortcoming and criticize them. This might lead to frustration. As a result they often do not cooperate with sales manager to achieve sales standards. This often leads to failure of the control system.

EXPENSIVE PROCESS: Sometimes the expenses incurred from using a control system is more than the benefits derived from it. This might in case of small organizations. It reduces the importance of control system.

## CONTINOUS CHANGE IN EXTERNAL

**ENVIRONMENTAL FACTORS:** External environmental factors keep on changing. For example economic condition, govt policy. Political situation, customer preferences, fashion and trend and level of competition keep on changing from time to time. Changes in these external factors lead to rendering of old standards futile. Standards fixed before may not be applicable in present scenario.

**DIFFICULTY IN FIXING INDIVIDUAL RESPONSIBILITY:** There are some sales activities which are performed by a group of salespersons. In such a case it is not possible to evaluate individual performance. This leads to difficulty in fixing individual evaluation criteria.

**DIFFICULTY IN FIXING STANDARDS:** Sales personnel are control and evaluated on the basis of existing standards but as it turns out it is very difficult to fix these standards. There are some activities for which standards cannot be determined, example-selling activities such as after sales service, enhancing customer satisfaction, servicing, etc. Another bottleneck is that standards are fixed even for future which is uncertain. Hence the standards which are set may be faulty and not up to the mark.

**INEFFICIENT CONTROLLERS:** The personnel who themselves engage in sales control system prove to be a problem. This may happen if the controllers themselves have less information to preset standards or they may not be expert in setting standards or they may make wrong assessment of actual level of salesmen. Also they might lack experience which leads to failure in exercising control. They may find the shortcomings in a wrong manner and as a result of it they may suggest the wrong remedial measure. This might lead to failure of the control system.

## SALES RECORDS AND REPORTING SYSTEM

Sales records are maintained by accounting department of sales Organization. These records are made on the basis of salesmen's reports. Salesmen send sales report of their sales territories periodically. Sales record includes information about:

- sales made,
- sales calls made,
- customer's complaints,
- selling expenses incurred,
- cash collected from customers,
- Discounts offered etc.

These records help the sales executives in sales planning, sales forecasting, sales control and in coordinating the activities of sales department with the other functional areas of management. Production schedules are prepared on the basis of sales records and sales forecasts.

Sales records are classified into two parts:

1) Sales and expense record
2) Records of other selling activities.

Sales and expense record include data regarding sales and selling expenses.

Sales records of other selling activities include:

- report regarding sales calls made,
- after sales services,
- customers complaints,
- Route plans of salesmen etc.

Sales records are made on the basis of sales reports. The sales reports are prepared by salesmen, field sales supervisor, territorial managers etc. At the grassroots these sales reports are prepared by the salesmen working in the sales territories. The salesmen are scattered over different sales-territories, in order to direct, manage and control the activities of salesmen. It is must for the sales managers to get information from the salesmen. This information can be with regard to sales in the sales territories and the problems that the salesmen are facing.

The sales manager should also know that whether the customers are satisfied with the products and services of the business unit, whether the dealers are cooperating with the salesmen, whether the sales-promotion schemes launched by the business unit are succeeding or not.

Salesman is the person who is actually in touch with customers and dealers and is working in sales territories. So he prepares a report about all these activities and sends it to the sales-manager regularly.

This report is an important source of information for the sales-manager. Information about competitive strategies and policies can be attained through these reports. The sales-manager can form or change his policies and programs on the basis of salesmen's reports. Similarly coordination between production and selling activities can be established on the basis of these reports. Through these reports, the sales manager can know the difficulties being faced by salesman. The sales manager can thus provide them timely assistance so that these difficulties will not affect the sales.

The sales manager can also evaluate the performance of individual salesman and can control their activities through the report of salesman.

## TYPES OF SALESMAN REPORT

Salesman report can be of various types. Main types are:

- Progress report/call Report
- Sales Complaint Report
- Loss of Business Report
- New Business Report
- Selling Expenses Report
- Future Work Plan Report

Each Report in detail is followed as:

1). Progress Report/Call Report:

Progress report is prepared by each salesman individually. It gives information about sales-call made by a salesman during a speci?c period. Such reports are prepared at regular interval of time. These reports give information about sales actually made, number of customers contacted, number of sales-order obtained etc. These reports help to evaluate performance of salesmen.

2). Sales Complaint Report:

This report gives information about complaints, objections, negative remarks made by customers/dealers. These complaints can be with regard to product quality, design, price, packaging, after-sales service etc. These complaint reports help the sales executives to identify weaknesses and defects of product, service. sales-programmes etc. By solving these complaints the level of satisfaction of customer/dealer can be enhanced.

3). Selling Expense Reports:

Salesperson incur various types of selling expenses like travelling expenses, boarding expenses, lodging expenses, entertainment expenses. etc. Salesmen are reimbursed these selling expenses by the business unit. Salesman have to report the amount, nature and purpose of these selling expenses periodically. These reports help the sales-executive in controlling wasteful selling expenses. The format of selling expense report is shown below:

**Selling Expenses Report**

Name of Salesman.......... Sales Territory...........

Time Period..........

| Day | Trave ling exp. | Boar ding exp. | Load ing exp. | Enterta inment exp. | Misc. exp. | Total exp. | Remarks |
|---|---|---|---|---|---|---|---|
| Monday | | | | | | | |
| Tuesday | | | | | | | |
| Wednesday | | | | | | | |
| Thursday | | | | | | | |
| Friday | | | | | | | |
| Saturday | | | | | | | |
| Total | | | | | | | |

4). Loss of Business Report:

This report provides information about loss of established customers. The salesman has to explain the reasons for loss of such customers. It helps the sales executives to modify sales-policies so that in future possible loss of customer is avoided. The higher authorities can make efforts to re-establish business relations with lost customers.

5). New Business Report:

This report provides information about new sales-areas, new customers, new dealers etc. For growth of business and to enlarge market share. It is necessary to contact new customers and enter new market areas.

6). Future Work Plan Report:

These reports are prepared by salesmen about their future work plan for a specific time period. These 'reports provide information about number of customers to be contacted, sales-route-plan, future travelling programs, areas to be visited etc. These reports help the sales executives to check the where-about of salesmen. These reports also help to timely evaluate the future route plans, travelling programs etc.

**Future Work Plan Report**

Name of Salesman.......... Sales Territory...........

Time Period..........

| Day | Name of Prospective Customer | Place | Purpose of Visit |
|---|---|---|---|
| | | ............ | ........... |
| Monday | | | |
| Tuesday | | | |
| Wednesday | | | |
| Thursday | | | |
| Friday | | | |
| Saturday | | | |
| Total | | | |

## REFERENCES / BIBLIOGRAPHY


- A Practical Approach to Sales Management
  By Kujnish Vashisht
- Advertising and Sales Management
  By Mukesh Trehan and Ranju Trehan
- http://www.wikipedia.org/
- http://en.wikipedia.org/wiki/Performance_appraisal
- http://www.businessdictionary.com/definition/performance-appraisal.html
- http://www.businessballs.com/performanceappraisals.htm
- http://en.wikipedia.org/wiki/Sales_operations
- http://www.businessdictionary.com/definition/sales-quota.html
- http://www.mbaskool.com/business-concepts/marketing-and-strategy-terms/1919-sales-quota.html
- http://www.journals.elsevier.com/performance-evaluation/